AQA A

Second Edition

A2

Claire Merrills

Jacqueline
Halls-Bryan

Nelson Thorr

Introduction

Nelson Thornes has worked hard to ensure this book and the accompanying online resources offer you excellent support for your A Level course. You can feel assured that they match the specification for this subject.

These print and online resources together **unlock blended learning**; this means that the links between the activities in the book and the activities online blend together to maximise your understanding of a topic and help you achieve your potential.

These online resources are available on 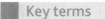 which can be accessed via the internet at **http://live.kerboodle.com**, anytime, anywhere. If your school or college subscribes to this service you will be provided with your own personal login details. Once logged in, access your course and locate the required activity.

For more information and help visit **http://www.kerboodle.com**

Icons in this book indicate where there is material online related to that topic. The following icons are used:

💡 Learning activity

These resources include a variety of interactive and non-interactive activities to support your learning. These include online presentations of concepts from the student book, online case studies and interactive activities.

☑ Progress tracking

These resources include a variety of tests that you can use to check your knowledge on particular topics (Test yourself) and a range of resources that enable you to analyse and understand examination questions (On your marks…).

¹²₃ Worked example

These resources provide step-by-step help on how to work through a particular accounting skill.

▮ How to use this book

The book content is divided into chapters and topics that match the AQA Accounting specification for Units 3 and 4. Chapters 1–8 cover Unit 3 and chapters 9–16 cover Unit 4.

The features in this book include:

In this chapter you will learn how to:

At the beginning of each section you will find a list of learning objectives that contain targets linked to the requirements of the specification.

Key terms

Terms that you will need to be able to define and understand.

■ Illustration

A worked example that will show you how to go through a particular accounting skill.

Case Study

An overarching business scenario, to be used throughout a topic or a chapter.

■ Activity

Suggestions for practical investigations you can carry out. These will help you to test your knowledge and understanding.

Background knowledge

An extension to the main text that will provide you with added bits of useful knowledge.

Links

This highlights any areas where topics relate to another part of this book or the AS specification.

Show the skills

Explanation of how a certain skill is relevant for further accounting study beyond A2 or in the wider world of work.

Study tip

Hints to help you with your study and to prepare for your exam.

Practice questions

Questions in the style that you can expect in your exam appear at the end of each topic and chapter. Answers for these are available online at **www.nelsonthornes.com/accounting**.

In this chapter you will have learnt:

A bulleted list of learning outcomes at the end of each chapter summarising core points of knowledge.

■ International standards

The accounting specification for AQA now includes the international terminology as set by the International Accounting Standards. These terms have been incorporated into this textbook to enable you to become familiar with their use. All of the past examination questions have been updated and rewritten using both the international term and the UK term. A table of the updates in terminology has been provided online at **www.nelsonthornes.com/accounting**.

■ Synoptic content

Remember that the A2 examinations will include a question with content that is synoptic with the AS specification. This means that subject content from the AS will be assessed again within an A2 examination paper. The case study and chapter questions may therefore contain content from both the AS and A2 specification.

■ Weblinks in the book

As Nelson Thornes is not responsible for third-party content online, there may be some changes to this material that are beyond our control. In order for us to ensure that the links referred to in the book are as up-to-date and stable as possible, the websites are usually homepages with supporting instructions on how to reach the relevant pages if necessary.

Please let us know at **kerboodle@nelsonthornes.com** if you find a link that doesn't work and we will do our best to redirect the link, or to find an alternative site.

Further aspects of financial accounting

◼ Introduction to Unit 3

Unit 3 is designed to develop your knowledge and understanding of financial accounting. You will find much of the work you undertook for the AS qualification will be of great value in this unit. For example, your understanding of accounting concepts and your ability to produce financial statements will prove invaluable as you develop skills in calculating the profit of businesses with limited accounting records, prepare accounting records for partnerships and study more advanced matters in relation to limited liability companies.

◼ Chapter 1 – Sources of finance

You will look at some commonly used sources of finance for businesses, including bank loans and overdrafts, shares, debentures and internal finance. You will be expected to assess these types of finance, making appropriate recommendations as to which source to choose in particular circumstances.

◼ Chapter 2 – Incomplete records

You will calculate the profits or losses of businesses that have not kept a full set of accounting records. You will learn a variety of techniques that are used to find the key information required to prepare financial statements under these circumstances. For example, you will learn how to calculate a business's credit sales when it has not maintained a sales day book or kept detailed records of trade receivables in a sales ledger.

◼ Chapter 3 – Partnership accounts introduction

This chapter will introduce you to the accounting records of partnerships. You will learn how partners keep individual records of their investment in a business, and some of the techniques that can be used to share profits and losses between the partners. You will study certain aspects of the Partnership Act 1890, and how this should be applied when partners have no agreement about how to share profits and losses.

◼ Chapter 4 – Partnership and change in partners

You will develop your skills in preparing partnership accounts. You will learn how to record the retirement of a partner and the admission of a new partner. For the first time, you will develop an understanding of an intangible asset, goodwill, and you will learn how adjustments are made for this asset when there is a change in partners. You will study how to record the dissolution of a partnership (that is how to close down a partnership business) and work out how much should be paid to each partner after assets have been sold and liabilities discharged.

Chapter 5 – Published accounts of limited companies

You will develop your understanding of the accounts of limited liability companies by identifying the main elements of their published reports. You will see why companies are required to publish their accounts, the benefits to various users, but also gain an appreciation of the limitations of this process. You will also look at the duties of directors and contrast these with the duties of auditors.

Chapter 6 – Statement of cash flows

You will focus on a particular aspect of published accounts, i.e. statements of cash flows. You will develop skills in preparing these statements following the requirements of the relevant International Accounting Standard (IAS 7). You will learn how to interpret statements of cash flows and how to assess the importance of these statements to others, particularly shareholders.

Chapter 7 – International Accounting Standards

You will learn about international accounting standards which are of great significance in ensuring that the financial statements prepared by companies are comparable, understandable and reliable. You will be looking at 10 of these standards and the focus will be on gaining an insight into the purpose and importance of each standard. You will not be expected to have a detailed knowledge of each standard (except IAS 7, which concerns statements of cash flows).

Chapter 8 – Inventory valuation

You will focus your attention on inventory. You will learn how to calculate inventory using two different methods, and you will also learn about the advantages and disadvantages of each of these methods. You will also learn to calculate a business's end of year inventory in situations where the valuation of the inventory has been delayed.

As you might expect, when you are assessed on this unit, you will be required to prepare financial statements, accounts, computations (i.e. annotated calculations). You will also, of course, be expected to write about accounting topics, providing explanations and reports in which you evaluate situations, giving advice and making recommendations. All the skills you developed preparing for the AS examination will now be very useful as you prepare for this module's assessment. For example, you will already know just how important it is to prepare accounting statements that are well presented and you will already have learned how to write effective explanations and reports. Do bear in mind, however, that many of the techniques you are mastering are more complex than those for the AS modules and that your prose answers will need to show a greater depth of understanding. Add to this the fact that, in general, higher standards are expected at A2 level.

1 Sources of finance

In this chapter you will learn how to:

- explain the advantages and disadvantages of a number of sources of finance (internal finance, shares, debentures, bank loans and overdrafts, and mortgages)

- apply understanding of types of finance to enable the most appropriate type of finance to be chosen in a particular situation

- evaluate different sources of finance and recommend the most appropriate choice to the owner(s) of a business.

Background information

Businesses require finance at all stages of their progress whatever their size and degree of success. As is often the case with individuals, the more successful a business, the easier it is to secure finance. Large, well-established businesses can borrow more and with better conditions attached, for example lower interest rates than would be available to a sole trader just starting out. Not all sources of finance are available to all types of businesses.

Key term

Internal finance: often the first source of finance for a business to consider and involves freeing up cash within the business.

The owners of businesses need to know the various sources of finance available in order to choose the one best suited to them and their situation. It is not necessarily the cheapest source of finance that is best. A business must consider the timescale involved and whether they are surrendering any control of the business in return for the finance. In order for you to be able to advise the owner(s) of the business about the different sources of finance and which is most appropriate, you need to understand what they are and the advantages and disadvantages of each source. Finance is needed for all sorts of reasons. At the start, finance will be needed to buy non-current assets such as machinery, computers or delivery vehicles. There will also be marketing and, possibly, training to carry out and it is very unlikely a new business would instantly secure credit facilities with suppliers so they need to ensure they have enough finance to buy all the inventory they require. Once they are more established they may want to set up additional outlets or expand overseas. All of these decisions require finance.

What is internal finance?

Internal finance is when the owner of a business looks within the business for possible sources of finance.

Table 1 *Sources of internal finance*

Improving cash inflows	Reducing cash outflows
- Tighter credit control; offer discounts for early payment and/or charge interest for late payment - Sell non-current assets that are no longer required	- Minimise wastage; how could this be done? - Tight inventory control, e.g. Just In Time (keeping inventory to a minimum and only replacing inventory as it is sold) - Delay paying trade payables where possible

Retaining profit is an obvious means of finance for those businesses doing well. Profit is a measure of the performance of the business assessed at the end of the financial year, but that profit will have been generated by revenue transactions over the course of that year. The cash generated from these revenue transactions though will have flowed into and out of the company on a daily basis. Hence whilst the business may have made substantial profits it does not mean that there is physical cash in place that mirrors this profit as profit itself is not real, it is a measurement only. For example, a business can have made a large profit but have spent cash on purchasing new non-current assets. The cost of the non-current assets is spread over their useful life using depreciation. Any successful business would be wise to reinvest some profit made back into net current assets and non-current assets.

What are the advantages of internal finance?

No interest is paid and there is no loss of control outside of the business. For example a loan may be secured against a non-current asset such as a vehicle that will be taken back by the company if the business cannot afford the repayments.

Any disadvantages?

- There may be insufficient amounts for what you need to do.
- May conflict with stakeholder wants. For example, shareholders want short-term profits for payment of dividends, managers want profit to be retained for investment and growth, employees may want profits to be used for pay rises or investment in training. Thus there are differing and diverse pressures relating to how any profits generated should be used.

■ Case study

Sources of finance for start-ups

Josie is a fitness fanatic and keen to set up her own gym just for women and strictly no mirrors. She has some savings and several friends and family who are supportive of her project. She is unsure where to get the finance required to buy the equipment she needs. She has found property (premises) to rent but would want to buy her own site in the long term so that she has more control over how she uses the building. If successful she believes that she could turn her business into a national chain.

■ Ordinary shares

Only private limited companies (Ltd) and public limited companies (plc) can issue (sell) shares. Private limited companies sell their shares to friends, family and employees and, as the word 'public' suggests, for plcs these can be sold to anyone. Shares can provide large amounts of finance, a lump sum cash injection that never needs to be repaid (permanent capital) and there is no need to pay **dividends**. However, you need to get your shareholders on your side if you decide not to pay dividends, and explain why. Perhaps you need the finance to buy new property (premises) that will result in higher profits in future years and subsequently larger dividends. If your shareholders are unconvinced by your reasoning then they may well sell their shares, which could ultimately lead to a fall in share value if enough of them did this. The actual company has no direct influence over share value as this is led by supply and demand for the shares. An alternative is to issue bonus shares that are free and can then be sold by the existing shareholders.

What are the advantages of ordinary shares?

If there is insufficient cash or profit or both then dividends do not have to be paid. Large amounts of money can be raised which does not have to be repaid.

What are the disadvantages of ordinary shares?

Loss of control: ordinary shareholders are the owners of the company. Some shareholders are not interested in the long-term future of the business and simply want to make a quick profit. This is why many businesses like their employees to own shares in the business because they will care about the future success. There is also the risk of takeover. This happens when a shareholder buys over 50% of the shares and so becomes the majority shareholder.

Preference shares

These shares have a preferential right to dividends over ordinary shareholders. This means that holders of preference shares will be paid their dividend first. They are considered to be lower risk for the investor because they are more likely to receive a dividend. However, their return is likely to be lower than that of an ordinary share. Holders of preference shares are not usually entitled to vote at the annual general meeting. **Preferences shares** can be cumulative or non-cumulative. If they are cumulative the dividend payout will build up even when there is no cash to pay out (this year it will be added to the following year). This means that if there is insufficient cash to pay out in one year, in the second year the shareholder will receive the first year's dividends plus the current second year's dividends. This does not happen with non-cumulative preference shares.

Activity

1 What are the advantages and disadvantages of preference shares for both the investor and the business?

Debentures

The most common error with **debentures** is that they are thought to be a type of share. They are actually a non-current loan and useful for financing projects that will take time to generate returns. The debenture holder lends the money for a fixed time period and a fixed amount of interest – for example, 7% debentures until 2025. This means that each year the debenture holder will receive 7% of the amount they have lent the company as interest and then in 2025 they will be repaid the original value in full. Debentures are useful when the business is certain they will then have the cash available in the necessary year to make the repayment as, unlike bank loans, only the interest is paid each year. Debenture interest is not optional and must be paid even when there is insufficient profit and/or cash. Debenture holders may be concerned about the risk they are taking in lending the money to the business, in which case the debentures are secured against the assets and the term 'mortgage' debenture is used. If the debentures are not secured they are simple or naked debentures.

Bank loans

Bank loans could be arranged for a medium term, up to 10 years or a long term over 10 years. This source of finance is often used to purchase non-current assets or for a specific project. The loan may be secured on the asset that has been bought with the funds raised by the loan and then if the business is unable to repay the loan this asset will be seized and used to pay the outstanding amount. Each month or year interest and part of the loan will be repaid. This can simplify budgeting as you know exactly how much you will be paying if the interest is fixed. Loans are not as flexible as overdrafts as you may not be able to make overpayments during times when you have surplus cash, and if you can then there may be a penalty charge involved.

Study tip

You need to make sure you are examining the source of finance from the correct viewpoint. This is particularly important when considering *risk*. From a business point of view ordinary shares may be low risk as they do not have to pay dividends whereas for the ordinary shareholder you may consider them fairly high risk as they may not get a return on their investment. A common error is for students to answer questions from, for example, the shareholders' perspective when the question was looking at finance from the business's viewpoint. Take time to read the question carefully to avoid this.

Key terms

Preference shares: for shareholders these are a lower risk option than ordinary shares but as a consequence offer a lower return.

Debentures: these are loans by debenture holders who receive interest for the term of the debenture. They must not be confused with shares.

Bank loans: borrowing a fixed sum over a fixed term which can be secured on assets in the business or unsecured. Interest must be paid in addition to the amount borrowed.

Show the skills

If you are asked to assess the suitable sources of finance for a business it is essential that, after having weighed up the pros and cons of the potential sources, you then reach a final decision and justify that. You may well decide that a combination of sources is best. If so, explain why.

Link

Types of business organisation is studied in AS Accounting (Unit 2).

Study tip

It is easier for both you and the examiner if you consider one source of finance at a time rather than completing advantages of them all and then revisiting them for the disadvantages.

Show the skills

Remember, some sources of finance will clearly be inappropriate for a business, such as a sole trader issuing shares, but in other circumstances there may be several possible sources that could be of use. You must match the source to its use.

■ Bank overdrafts

A **bank overdraft** is the most common type of short-term finance. It provides useful cash and is often the cheapest form of borrowing as, although the interest rate is usually higher than a bank loan, you are only charged interest when actually overdrawn. It is essential that a close eye is kept on the limit set as banks will charge higher interest and fees for exceeding it. Although we consider overdrafts as short term many businesses are frequently overdrawn each month if their cash flow is not always consistent. Overdrafts are often used for day-to-day expenses rather than large capital expenditure and are seen by many businesses as a safety net. They are flexible as they can be repaid when the business wants.

■ Mortgages

Mortgages are obtained for purchasing property (premises). The amount lent and the interest rate will vary according to the property (premises) involved and the financial record of the business. They are a non-current liability and usually a relatively cheap source of finance. They are particularly useful for smaller businesses who may struggle to borrow elsewhere as a mortgage is secured against their property (premises) making it a lower risk for the lender, who can repossess (take back the property (premises) by force using a court order) if the borrower defaults.

Activities

2 In groups you need to split the sources of finance between you and research what they are and the advantages and disadvantages of each. You can then compile a group handout of your findings. Evaluate which would be the best sources for Josie starting her gym. She intends to start as a sole trader.

3 Imran, an old friend from college, has approached Josie as he thinks she has found a new and expanding market and wants to join her. What sources of finance could now be available?

■ Risks in being a lender or borrower

Risk is important to both the lender and borrower. The lender or investor wants to ensure they receive a return on their funds and ultimately repayment. The business, in the role of borrower, wants an affordable option but also the source of finance to be in a form and length of time appropriate for their needs. The business also needs to weigh up factors like losing control, for example, by issuing **ordinary shares**. Shareholders usually want to see a good return on their investment whilst the original owners may wish to use retained profit to expand the business further, for example by buying additional non-current assets. Most businesses will require sources of finance at some stage of their existence. What you need to examine is the type of business, what the finance is being used for and the financial situation the business finds itself in.

In this chapter you will have learnt:

- the advantages and disadvantages that arise from each of the sources of finance
- to apply understanding of each source so as to be able to choose the most appropriate source of finance for a particular situation.

Practice questions

1   Distinguish between debentures and ordinary shares.

2   Harvey and Bailey are in partnership. Explain the additional sources of finance they could benefit from by becoming a limited company.

3   Creamy Smoothies Ltd want to expand into the European market. They have two factories, a healthy profit from the past year and approximately £5,000 cash at bank. They estimate they require £125,000 for their plans. Discuss how best they should raise the finance.

4   Discuss the possible conflict that may exist between the managers and shareholders of a company when raising finance.

5   AQA ACC3 January 2013
     Evans and Schleck have agreed to start a new business as a private limited company. The business will require start-up funds of £250,000. Evans and Schleck will invest a total of £100,000. They are considering raising the additional capital required through the issuing of shares. They believe that profits will be low during the first year of trading.

     Assess the suitability of a share issue to raise the start-up capital required by Evans and Schleck.

Study tip

In an examination you would receive marks for the quality of your written communication.

2 Incomplete records

This chapter prepares you to answer incomplete records questions that often appear daunting as it can be difficult to assess what information is of use to you and where it should be placed. In the first topic we will start by looking at why incomplete records occur and how a statement of affairs can be produced to help calculate profit or loss without the need to complete an income statement (second section). Incomplete records are more common in businesses owned by sole traders but they also could occur in partnerships. The second topic, preparing financial statements for businesses with incomplete records, brings together previous techniques you have completed at AS level. It is possible to produce a set of financial statements without a complete trial balance and you will learn how to do this by the end of this chapter.

Topic 1 Calculating profits and losses from changes in capital

In this topic you will learn how to:

- assess the profit or loss made by a business that has minimal accounting records based on a comparison of the value of capital at two different dates

- evaluate a system of incomplete records based on comparing capitals comparing this with full accounting systems.

Explanatory note

As a result of the changes in terminology relating to the different sections of income statements, the income statement (trading account) will be referred to as the 'income statement (first section)'. This includes from revenue to gross profit. The income statement (profit and loss account) will now be referred to as the 'income statement (second section)'. This includes from gross profit to profit (or loss) for the year.

■ The reasons for incomplete records

Incomplete records range from partially completed accounts to a list of assets and a pile of bank statements. A sole trader or partnership often has neither the time nor expertise to keep a double-entry bookkeeping system. Preparing accounting statements is essential for tax purposes and for making effective management decisions. With the price of computers and software packages specifically for accounts becoming more cost effective, it is increasingly easier for a non-accountant to keep basic records. This will then keep accountancy fees lower when the end of year financial statements need to be prepared.

Limited companies would usually employ a bookkeeper and larger companies have whole departments with a range of accounting staff, but – although keeping financial records – these employees may not have the qualifications to produce a full set of financial statements. Many accounting software packages are generic, so unless the business pays for a tailor-made package the system may only complete some of the required record keeping. Some sole traders might use a single-entry system. This involves recording all payments, receipts and other transactions in one cash book. This is helpful but we still need to draw out items such as drawings and capital expenditure. Capital expenditure, spending or improving on non-current assets means that we need to calculate depreciation. Adjustments for trade payables and trade receivables will also need to be made, as well as other receivables (prepayments) and other payables (accruals).

Advantages of maintaining limited accounting records

- Simple and easy to do, particularly for small businesses that may not have financial expertise.

- Do not need to hire a permanent fully qualified accountant.
- Do not need expensive tailor-made accounting software.

Statement of affairs

In order to calculate the capital at the beginning of the financial year, we use the accounting equation:

assets – liabilities = capital

Statement of Affairs for J. Wimpenny at 1 January 2013

	£	£
Assets		
Machinery		10,000
Inventory		2,000
Trade receivables		1,000
Bank		5,500
		18,500
Liabilities		
Trade payables	3,500	
Other payables (accruals)	500	4,000
Capital		**14,500**

Fig. 2.1 *An example of a statement of affairs*

Total assets – total liabilities = capital

18,500 – 4,000 = £14,500

So, we can calculate that at 1 January 2013, J. Wimpenny had £14,500 invested in his business.

It is a useful to complete a **statement of affairs** if we do not have a statement of financial position (balance sheet) for the previous year.

Case study

Sundip Patel

Sundip Patel is a games software designer who is involved in generating the backgrounds on virtual online games. He enjoys his work and although he is more than capable of maintaining accounting records he considers it to be a waste of his time. Sundip is starting to have to turn away projects because he is unable to keep up with the demand for his service.

Using a statement of affairs to calculate profit or loss

It is possible to calculate profit without an income statement (second section). Unless capital has been introduced, the only way capital can

Show the skills

Solving incomplete records problems draws together a whole range of accounting skills from your studies. The reality of having sole traders and partnerships as clients for an accountant is the fact that their clients' accounting knowledge may be very limited or indeed non-existent. Accountants need to encourage sole traders and partnerships to keep all source documents (which you studied in AS Unit 1) so that accurate accounting records can then be created. It is important to closely examine all the evidence the client produces and discover the gaps. Double-entry, control accounts, ratio analysis and completing financial statements are all the skills brought together in order to produce profit figures which can be used for tax purposes and for decision making.

increase over the year is by profit being earned. You need to first calculate the opening and closing capital balances using two statements of affairs, for the start and the end of the year, and then you are able to compare them to find any increase or decrease in capital that would represent profit or loss made over the period.

Illustration

Calculating profit or loss using opening and closing capital

Assets or liabilities	At 30 March 2012	At 30 March 2013
Property (premises)	100,000	120,000
Vehicles	30,000	25,000
Inventory	2,000	2,500
Trade receivables	1,800	1,950
Trade payables	880	1,020
Non-current bank loan	20,000	18,000

Fig. 2.2 *Assets and liabilities*

Sundip Patel presented us with the above information. The opening capital at 30 March 2012 is £112,920. We find this by totalling the assets (100,000 + 30,000 + 2,000 + 1,800) and then subtracting the liabilities (880 + 20,000). If we do the same for 2013 we find the closing capital to be £130,430: assets (120,000 + 25,000 + 2,500 + 1,950) £149,450 less liabilities (1,020 + 18,000) £19,020.

Closing capital − opening capital = profit or loss

£130,430 − £112,920 = £17,510 profit

However, it is likely that the owner will have had drawings of either inventory or cash during the year and possibly have introduced additional capital. In this case we need to adjust capital using a layout such as the following one:

	£
Closing capital	
Less opening capital	
Add drawings	
Less capital introduced	
Profit for the year	

Fig. 2.3 *Adjusting capital*

Activity

 Complete the above table using Sundip's previous information. He has also introduced £5,000, which was an inheritance, and has drawings of £10,000.

Assessment: using a statement of affairs to calculate profit or loss

This is a quick method to discover profit or loss without completing an income statement. It is accurate as long as the figures provided are accurate, such as the trade receivables, trade payables, inventory, etc.

Drawbacks

1 The method is not detailed enough for management purposes.
2 It would not be sufficient for income tax and VAT purposes.

Activity

5 Sundip's friend is a trainee accountant and considers that Sundip should complete a full set of accounting records in order to calculate profit or loss rather than comparing opening and closing capitals. Advise Sundip as to whether his friend is correct.

In this topic you will have learnt:

- how to prepare a statement of affairs and calculate profit or loss from changes in capital over time
- how to assess the drawbacks of maintaining limited accounting records.

Practice questions

1   Explain the purpose of a statement of affairs.

2   Dermot Reegan is a car mechanic and supplies you with the following information:

	1 January 2013 £	31 December 2013 £
Property (premises)	120,000	120,000
Vehicles	50,000	60,000
Machinery	12,000	30,000
Bank	1,300	1,800
Cash	500	650
Trade payables	2,000	1,800
Trade receivables	3,300	3,750
Inventory	1,200	1,500

Calculate the profit or loss for the year taking into account Dermot's drawings of £10,000.

3   Khurram does not keep full books of account. He has provided the following information.

Assets and liabilities

	Opening balances at 31 March 2012 £	Closing balances at 31 March 2013 £
Bank overdraft	3,000	1,750
Cash in hand	150	200
Vehicles at net book value	5,685	4,658
Rent paid in advance	450	550
Inventory	6,240	5,670
Wages accrued	350	425
Trade payables	2,857	3,857
Trade receivables	3,410	2,950

Cash drawings of £10,000 for the year ending 31 March 2013.

Prepare statements of affairs to calculate the profit or loss for the year ended 31 March 2013.

4   Jasmine started a bridal-wear business on 1 December 2012 with net assets valued at £52,000. She has been very busy building her business so has not bothered with financial records, but she can provide the following information at 30 November 2013.

	£
Property (premises) at valuation	62,000
Van at net book value	4,000
Trade payables	6,545
Trade receivables	5,225
Bank overdraft	2,000
Cash	500
Non-current loan	3,500
Inventory	20,000

During the year Jasmine withdrew £8,250 cash for herself. She also got married and took a dress worth £1,500.
(a)   Calculate her profit or loss for the year ended 30 November 2013.
(b)   Assess the method that you used to determine the profit or loss.

5   Rebecca Chappell owns a children's nursery and supplies the following information:

	31 December 2012	31 December 2013
Property (premises)	120,000	130,000
Equipment	10,000	15,000
Cash	1,000	1,500
Bank	2,225	3,800
Inventory	275	122
Receivables	987	1,030
Other receivables (prepayments)	250	300
Payables	760	550

During the year ended 31 December 2013 Rebecca introduced her bingo winnings of £2,500 and took £80 worth of inventory home for her own children's use.

Calculate Rebecca's profit or loss for the year ended 31 December 2013.

Topic 2   Preparing financial statements for businesses with incomplete records

In this topic you will learn how to:

- prepare the financial accounts of a business that has incomplete accounting records

- use a variety of techniques to calculate key figures for inclusion in the financial statements of a business that has incomplete accounting records

- use more advanced techniques to calculate missing cash or inventory

- evaluate this system of incomplete records comparing it with full accounting systems.

■ Credit sales and credit purchases

Cash sales and purchases can usually be calculated by looking at the cash book, till rolls and receipts. However, when calculating credit sales and purchases, receivable balances and payable balances must be taken account of at both the beginning and end of the year.

Essential information to calculate credit sales and credit purchases

Table 1 *Information required*

Credit sales	Credit purchases
Opening balance of trade receivables	Opening balance of trade payables
Closing balance of trade receivables	Closing balance of trade payables
Receipts from trade receivables	Payments to trade payables

We can calculate credit sales and credit purchases by completing a sales ledger or purchase ledger control account with the known information and then calculating the missing figures. It might also be necessary to consider: discounts received, discounts allowed, bad debts, returns inwards, returns outwards, interest charged to trade receivables or finance costs (interest payable) charged by trade payables.

Link

Sales ledger and purchase ledger control accounts were studied in AS Unit 1.

Illustration

How to set out a sales ledger control account or sales totals account

Dr			Sales ledger control account					Cr
			£					£
Dec	1	Bal b/d	20,000	Dec	31	Receipts from receivables		62,000
	31	**Sales**	**86,050**		31	Sales returns		2,000
	31	Interest charged	1,000		31	Discounts allowed		3,250
					31	Bad debts		500
					31	Bal c/d		39,300
			107,050					107,050
Jan	1	Bal b/d	39,300					

Fig. 2.4 *Sales ledger control account*

Remember that the opening receivables balance is a DEBIT, as it is an asset. Entries on the debit side increase the amount the receivables owe you. The control account is then completed and the total of credit sales from the sales day book can be calculated by filling in the missing figure. In this case the missing sales figure is £86,050.

A purchase ledger control account or purchase totals account is used to find credit purchases, see below:

Dr			Purchase ledger control account					Cr
			£					£
Dec	31	Payments to trade payables	93,500	Dec	1	Bal b/d		62,000
	31	Purchase returns	3,000		31	**Purchases**		**112,500**
	31	Discounts received	4,200		31	Interest paid		990
	31	Bal c/d	74,790		31			
			175,490					175,490
				Jan	1	Bal b/d		74,790

Fig. 2.5 *Purchase ledger control account*

This time the balance brought down is CREDIT, as it is a liability. Again, total credit purchases from the purchases day book can be calculated. In this case the missing figure is £112,500.

Calculating missing figures using markup or margin

Many businesses, especially sole traders, use a simple system of adding a set percentage markup to their goods or services so they know that

Study tip

Remember, cash sales and cash purchases are not entered in control accounts as these items do not affect trade receivables and trade payables.

they are making a profit margin on everything they sell. We can use this information to calculate sales or the cost of sales if these figures are not supplied. The important distinction to make here is that margin is a percentage profit based on the selling price, and markup is based on the cost of sales.

Markup

This is when a set percentage is added to the cost to generate the sales value.

Illustration

If you know the cost of sales and the markup is 10%:

£60,000 + 10% of cost of sales = £66,000 sales

If you know the sales and want to find the cost of

sales, then $\dfrac{66,000}{1.1}$ = £60,000 cost of sales

If the percentage was 20% then you would divide by 1.2 and so on.

Illustration

How to prepare an income statement (first section)

Dawid Jurkiewicz runs a joke shop selling a range of items. The following information is given on 30 November 2013.

Opening inventory at cost	£50,000
Markup on cost	20%
Rate of inventory turnover	8 times
Closing inventory	£55,000

Fig. 2.6 *Information supplied*

You are required to prepare the income statement (first section) for the year ended 30 November 2013.

Income statement (first section) for Dawid Jurkiewicz for the year ended 30 November 2013

		£	£
Revenue			504,000
Less	**Cost of sales**		
	Opening inventory	50,000	
	Purchases	425,000	
	Closing inventory	55,000	
			420,000
	Gross profit		84,000

Fig. 2.7 *Income statement (first section) to show markup method*

Start by entering the information that you are sure about, which is the opening and closing inventory. We can then use the rate of inventory turnover to calculate the cost of sales.

$$\text{Cost of sales} = \left(\frac{\text{opening inventory} + \text{closing inventory}}{2}\right) \times \text{inventory turnover}$$

$$\text{So, } 420,000 = \left(\frac{50,000 + 55,000}{2}\right) \times 8$$

Then add the closing inventory of £55,000 to the cost of sales of £420,000 and subtract the opening inventory of £50,000 to find the purchases of £425,000. To find the gross profit calculate 20% of the cost of sales £420,000, which is £84,000, and add the two amounts together to find the revenue of £504,000.

Margin

This is when a fixed percentage profit margin is made on every sale, i.e. 10% is profit and 90% of the revenue made is cost of sales, so revenue × 0.9 = cost of sales.

Illustration

If you know the revenue is £90,000 and the margin is 10% then:

£90,000 × 10% = £9,000 profit

Cost of sales is the revenue – profit = £90,000 = £81,000

Alternatively, £90,000 – 10% = £81,000; this is the same as £90,000 × 0.9 = £81,000

So, if you know the cost of sales and the fixed percentage profit margin, you can work out the revenue:

$$\frac{81,000}{0.9} = £90,000 \text{ revenue}$$

To obtain the 0.9 think about 10% subtracted from 100% and put a decimal point in, so, 20% converts to 0.8.

Illustration

Philip Taylor owns a surf shop in Newquay. The following information is given on 31 July 2013.

Revenue	£100,000
Gross profit margin	40%
Rate of inventory turnover	20 times
Opening inventory	£5,000

Fig. 2.8 *Information supplied*

You are required to prepare the income statement (first section) for the year ended 31 July 2013.

Income statement (first section) for Philip Taylor for the year ended 31 July 2013

		£	£
Revenue			100,000
Less	**Cost of sales**		
	Opening inventory	5,000	
	Purchases	56,000	
	Closing inventory	1,000	
			60,000
	Gross profit		40,000

Fig. 2.9 *Income statement (first section) to show margin method*

Again, start by entering the information that you are sure about, which is the opening inventory and revenue. This time use the revenue figure to calculate gross profit by finding 40% of revenue, which is £40,000. Subtract the gross profit from the revenue to find cost of sales of £60,000.

$$\text{Cost of sales} = \left(\frac{\text{opening inventory} + \text{closing inventory}}{2}\right) \times \frac{\text{inventory}}{\text{turnover}}$$

$$\text{So } 60,000 = \left(\frac{5,000 + \text{closing inventory}}{2}\right) \times 20$$

Divide £60,000 by 20 to find £3,000, which represents the average inventory, so closing inventory must be £1,000 so that 5,000 + 1,000 divided by 2 is £3,000. To find purchases start with the cost of sales of £60,000, add the closing inventory of £1,000 and subtract the opening inventory of £5,000.

Inventory losses

If inventory is lost because of fire or theft then it must be valued in order to make an insurance claim or account for the loss on the financial statements. Even if inadequate inventory records were kept we can still value the inventory loss by constructing an income statement (first section) and using the markup or margin technique.

■ Illustration

Kay owns a balloon shop in the local high street and on 21 May there was a fire that destroyed most of her inventory. She could salvage £500 worth and the insurance assessor requires an accurate assessment of inventory loss on the claim form.

At the start of the financial year Kay had an opening inventory value of £6,000. Her purchases to 21 May had been £28,000. Her revenue to this date was £40,000, Kay has a margin of 25% on sales.

Show the skills

Extract the figures you definitely know when completing an incomplete records question and then look for the gaps you need to complete.

■ Activities

6 Calculate the revenue and gross profit if the cost of sales is £360,000 with a 20% markup.

7 Calculate the cost of sales and gross profit if the revenue is £20,000 with a 25% markup.

8 Calculate the cost of sales and gross profit if the revenue is £400,000 with a gross profit margin of 25%.

9 Calculate the revenue and gross profit if the cost of sales is £260,000 with a 35% gross profit margin.

Income statement (first section) for Kay for the period ended 21 May 2013

		£	£
Revenue			40,000
Less	**Cost of sales**		
	Opening inventory	6,000	
	Purchases	28,000	
	Closing inventory	**4,000**	30,000
	Gross profit		10,000

Fig. 2.10 *Income statement (first section) to show loss of inventory*

So, if revenue = £40,000 and sales margin = 25% then gross profit = £10,000. If revenue = £40,000 and profit was £10,000 then the cost of sales = £30,000. From this we can now find the missing figure representing the inventory Kay should have had. This is done by calculating what closing inventory should have been by laying our information out in an income statement (first section). We can see that the closing inventory should have been £4,000 and if Kay now has only £500 worth of inventory left then £3,500 was lost in the fire.

Study tip

Preparing financial statements from incomplete records is one of the most challenging elements in the entire specification. It is advisable to spend some time developing the skills required by practising techniques using a range of questions.

In the income statement (first section), when calculating the cost of sales, the closing inventory must include any missing inventory so that gross profit can be calculated. The missing inventory should not be included on the statement of financial position (balance sheet) as we do not have it so it cannot be an asset. If Kay is not insured then missing inventory is written off as an expense on the income statement (second section). If she does have adequate insurance then it will appear as a current asset on the statement of financial position (balance sheet) until the insurance company pays her.

Calculation of missing cash

Exam questions sometimes require you to calculate a cash figure due to a theft. The key here is to prepare a cash account based on what should have happened and then compare it with the actual position.

Illustration

Sundip Patel does not keep a full set of accounting records. Whilst in a café-bar after visiting several clients Sundip had his briefcase stolen containing cash that he was on his way to deposit at the bank, but he was unsure of how much. He can provide the following information:

	£
Cash balance at 1 July 2012	278
Cash balance at 30 June 2013	145
Cash sales for the year	34,525
Cash paid into the bank during the year	30,250
Expenses paid by cash	2,870

Fig. 2.11 *Information supplied*

Dr			Cash					Cr
			£					£
June	30	Bal b/d	278	June	30	Bank		30,250
	30	Sales	34,525		30	Expenses		2,870
					30	**Stolen**		**1,538**
					30	Bal c/d		145
			34,803					34,803
July	1	Bal b/d	145					

Fig. 2.12 *Cash account*

By completing all the known figures first, we can then work out how much has been stolen from Sundip. In this case the figure is £1,538.

Stages in completing financial statements from incomplete records

The approach will vary according to the information given:

1   If you do know the assets and liabilities at the start or end of the year then you can complete a statement of affairs in order to calculate the opening and/or closing capital.

2   When completing control accounts, be careful – payments to trade payables and receipts from trade receivables do not represent sales and purchases. You must take into account opening and closing trade receivables and trade payables.

3   Use markup or margin as appropriate; markup is based on cost of sales and margin is based on sales.

4   If you are told inventory turnover then you can use this to calculate the cost of sales:

$$\text{Cost of sales} = \left(\frac{\text{opening inventory + closing inventory}}{2}\right) \times \frac{\text{inventory}}{\text{turnover}}$$

Revenue can also be found by applying any markup or margin information to the cost of sales figure.

5   Draw up the outline of the financial statements and include as much information as you can find remembering to take account of other payables (accruals) and other receivables (prepayments), adjustments to drawings etc. For example, last year's other payables (accruals) should have been paid last year and so need subtracting and this year's other payables (accruals) need adding. Ask yourself what costs and revenues actually happened in this accounting period rather than when were they paid. Remember profit is calculated using the other payables (accruals) concept. Include both cash sales and credit sales in the revenue figure and the same for purchases.

Benefits and drawbacks of maintaining a double-entry bookkeeping system

Whilst acknowledging the need for professional accountants who are crucial for areas other than producing financial statements, such as tax advice and the development of your business, it is increasingly possible due to computing packages for more detailed accounting records to be kept by non-specialists.

Study tip

Don't forget to include the cash and/or bank account when calculating opening or closing capital amounts as these are sometimes shown separately to the other information.

Link

In AS Unit 1 you will have learnt how to perform a bank reconciliation. This could be useful for an incomplete records question where perhaps the bank balance is unknown due to a lack of cash book and should be revised.

Link

Gross profit margin, markup and rate of inventory turnover were all studied as part of AS Unit 2.

Study tip

You must show detailed workings on your answer paper and not on the exam paper. There are marks available which you should maximise.

Table 2 *Benefits and drawbacks of maintaining a double-entry bookkeeping system*

Benefits	Drawbacks
Helps to support loan applications	May need to employ a bookkeeper
Less errors due to each entry having a debit and credit	Time consuming and less time to run the business
Provides information for tax purposes to pay HM Revenue and Customs	Not all errors will be revealed (remember the six errors for Unit 1)
Easy to produce trial balances at regular intervals	There is no statutory requirement for a sole trader to keep accounting records
Reduces fees paid to accountants	

In this topic you will have learnt:

- how to calculate credit sales and purchases figures using total control accounts
- how to calculate missing figures using markup or margin
- how to prepare and comment on financial statements based on incomplete records.

Practice questions

1   Max Turner is a sole trader and operates as an antiques dealer. The following details relate to his business for the year ended 31 March 2013.

Revenue	£900,000
Gross profit margin	25%
Rate of inventory turnover	10 times
Opening inventory	£40,000

Prepare the trading section of the income statement for the year ended 31 March 2013.

2   Miranda Ericson operates as a retailer selling toys and gifts. The following details relate to her business for the year ended 30 September 2013.

Opening inventory	£35,000
Markup on cost	20%
Rate of inventory turnover	8 times
Closing inventory	£25,000

Prepare the trading section of the income statement for the year ended 30 September 2013.

3   Vicky Hoang does not keep a full set of accounting records. Three days before her financial year end an amount is stolen from the business. Vicky provides you with the following information.

	£
Cash balance at 1 April 2012	369
Cash balance at 31 March 2013	140
Expenses paid by cash	18,451
Cash paid into the bank	285,460
Cash sales	305,451

(a)   Calculate the amount of cash missing on 31 March 2013.

(b)   Advise Vicky on two measures she could use to prevent such a loss occurring in the future.

4   Kia Ng has not kept adequate records for his business for the year ended 30 June 2013. He has supplied the following information.

Markup on cost	25%
Amount paid to trade payables	£363,000
Business expenses (excluding depreciation)	£52,100
Drawings	£20,500

	30 June 2012	30 June 2013
Vehicle	12,000	10,000
Cash at bank	3,300	12,075
Trade payables	8,000	6,500
Inventory	6,000	12,000
Prepaid business expenses	220	450

(a)   Prepare the income statement for the year ended 30 June 2013.

(b)   Prepare a statement of financial position (balance sheet) at 30 June 2013.

(c)   Evaluate Kia Ng's current system of maintaining incomplete accounting records.

5   AQA ACC3 January 2012

Alberto does not keep full accounts. However, the following information has been obtained for the year ended 31 December 2011.

Bank account			
Dr			Cr
Bal b/d at 1 Jan 2011	2,950	Payments to trade payables	38,990
Cash banked	13,095	Wages	24,895
Receipts from trade receivables	47,220	Payments for non-current assets	8,500
Proceeds from sale of non-current assets	5,890		
Bal c/d at 31 Dec 2011	3,230		
	72,385		72,385

Key terms

Deed of partnership: this is a legal document. Ideally all partnerships should have one of these so they know exactly how profits will be shared etc.

Interest on capital: this is an appropriation of the profits of the partnership and rewards those partners who have invested most.

Partnership salary: this is a payment to a partner and appears in the appropriation section, not with expenses. It is also entered in the partner's current account. It may reflect that some partners may contribute more working hours than others.

Interest on drawings: in order to deter partners from taking excessive drawings there may be interest charged that is then debited to the partners' accounts.

Partnership Act 1890: this states, for example, how to share profits or losses if no agreement is in place.

Partnership agreements

It is usual for a partnership to draw up a written agreement such as a **deed of partnership** which sets out the terms and financial arrangements. This avoids disagreements at a later stage. This is a legally binding document.

Possible contents of a partnership agreement

In addition to the obvious information such as personal details of the partners, the decision-making process, working hours, etc., the following should be considered when drawing up a partnership agreement:

1 Capital introduced – how much each partner is required to contribute to the business.
2 Profit/loss sharing ratio – this is how the partners share the profits or losses and can be done according to who works the most hours, who is the most skilled, who contributed most capital, etc.
3 **Interest on capital** – this is interest paid to the partners according to how much capital they have invested. The more they have invested, the more interest they receive. This reduces the amount of profit in the partnership but improves the individual partner's current account.
4 **Partnership salaries** – it may be agreed that some partners receive a salary in addition to their share of the profit or loss. This could be to ensure a partner receives a minimum income, perhaps because they left a lucrative salary with a company to join the partnership.
5 Drawings and **interest on drawings** – drawings is the amount that the partners withdraw from the partnership. Interest may be charged in order to minimise the amount removed. A serious cash shortage could be caused if one or more partners draws out a significant amount of cash.
6 Guarantees – if one partner guarantees that another will earn a minimum income in the business, such a guarantee should be written into the agreement.
7 Interest on loans – a partner may wish to lend the partnership finance as this may incur less interest than borrowing from a financial institution.

If no partnership agreement exists then the **Partnership Act 1890** comes into effect, which states that:

- profits and losses are shared equally
- there are no partners' salaries
- partners are entitled to 5% interest on any loans advanced to the business
- partners should not receive any interest on capital
- no interest is charged on drawings.

Case study

Wenches with Wrenches

Bonnie is a plumber operating as a sole trader who has captured a niche market in Guildford by completing jobs for women who would rather have another woman in their house to complete work needed. She has become very successful by completing jobs in the designated time frame and has a good reputation for tidying up after herself. She is having to turn jobs away and has been approached by Lucinda, a young woman who has just completed her plumbing qualifications, with the offer of a partnership.

Activities

 1 Discuss whether Bonnie should enter into partnership with Lucinda.

2 Outline what details they should have in their partnership agreement.

Fixed capital accounts

Some partnerships may have fluctuating capital accounts where all entries associated with the actual partners are recorded. This does not reveal if one partner is drawing out considerably more than the others. This can be a particular problem if the partnership is experiencing cash flow difficulties. The **fixed capital account** shows the original amounts that the individual partners have contributed and is only amended if a partner introduces or withdraws substantial amounts, this could be cash or assets. This usually only takes place by agreement with the other partners. It is possible with the dissolution (ending) of a partnership for a partner to have a debit balance in the capital account. This will be dealt with in a later topic.

The main advantages of keeping fixed capital accounts is that it is easy to determine the current investment position of any partner and to calculate interest on capital.

Debit	Credit
Capital withdrawn (cash/other assets)	Bal b/d (opening capital balance)
Goodwill written off	Capital introduced (cash/other assets)
Bal c/d (closing capital balance)	Goodwill created

Fig. 3.1 *Contents of a fixed capital account*

Goodwill represents the reputation, client base and success of the partnership thus far and rewards the existing partners in the old profit sharing ratio. It is an intangible asset so will normally be amortised (written off) from the statement of financial position (balance sheet) in the new profit sharing ratio. It can also be the difference between the worth of the partnership, the net assets and how much the partnership could be sold for.

Current accounts

A **current account** is used for the partners to record their share of profits or losses, salaries, total drawings and any interest on drawings or capital. The opening balance could either be a debit or a credit. A debit balance signifies that a partner has withdrawn more money than he or she is entitled to and, therefore, is in debt to the firm. A credit balance signifies that the partners have increased the level of their current investment in the partnership. A close eye should be kept on current accounts. It is important for cash flow purposes that the partners do not withdraw too much as then additional overdrafts and loans, which incur interest, could be needed.

The main advantage of keeping separate fluctuating current accounts is that this makes it immediately apparent if any partner is taking more in drawings than they are making in total appropriation of profits, that is, if they are eroding their personal capital position.

Importance of current accounts

Current accounts are a useful part of partnership accounts. For the benefit of all partners involved an accurate record must be kept of drawings made, interest on capital or drawings, partnership salaries and appropriated profits and losses. Remember that major changes in actual capital movements are kept separately in a fixed capital account as far as we are concerned for the examination. If we were to merge the two accounts it would make it more difficult to calculate interest on capital and also to recognise when a partner is continually drawing out more than they should be and depleting their capital injection. Capital

Key terms

Fixed capital accounts: the amount of capital introduced or withdrawn by each partner is recorded in a separate account and does not alter unless agreed by the partnership.

Goodwill: reflects the reputation built up by a partnership, this is an intangible asset and there are several different approaches to valuing it, but it is essentially a reflection of the success of the partnership. This could be based on previous profits for example. It could also represent the difference between the net assets of the partnership and the amount the partnership could be sold for.

Current account: records all the partners' drawings, interest on drawings, interest on capital, partnership salaries and shares of residual profit or loss.

Study tip

The opening balance on the capital account is always credit. Think CC, Credit Capital, to remember this.

Study tip

When goodwill is written off it may be helpful to think of it as being 'destroyed', DD, Debit Destroyed goodwill.

Study tip

To help you remember the layout for a current account remember LID (loss, interest on drawings, drawings) and SIP (salaries, interest on capital and profit). Interest on drawings is entered on the same side as drawings.

Study tip

Prepare current accounts in the columnar form, with all partners as shown in this chapter. It will save you time in the exam.

Activity

3 What are the advantages of maintaining separate current and capital accounts for Bonnie and Lucinda?

Link

Look back at income statements for sole traders which you studied as part of AS Unit 1. Partnership financial statements are very similar to those of a sole trader.

and current accounts both represent the amounts owed to the partners. Current accounts take the short-term view whereas capital accounts are long-term and are only affected by permanent change. A partner may decide to move funds between their current and capital accounts, especially if there is a closing debit balance on their current account.

Illustration

Example of a current account

Dr			Current Account		Cr
	B	L		B	L
Bal b/d	5,500		Bal b/d		12,200
Interest on drawings	800	900	Salaries	15,000	15,000
Drawings	18,500	24,400	Interest on capital	1,000	800
			Profit	6,000	6,000
Bal c/d		8,700	Bal c/d	2,800	
	24,800	34,000		24,800	34,000
Bal b/d	2,800		Bal b/d		8,700

Fig. 3.2 *An example of a current account for the two partners Bonnie and Lucinda*

The balances brought down at the start reveal that Bonnie owes the partnership £5,500 whilst the partnership owes Lucinda £12,200. Bonnie continues to withdraw more than she is entitled to as shown by the closing balance brought down which is a debit balance. Lucinda has not made drawings in excess of the salary and interest on capital built up and still has a credit balance of £8,700.

Appropriation accounts

Key term

Appropriation account: this account records the distribution of profits among partners based on any agreement made by the partners. Where there is no agreement the terms of the Partnership Act 1890 should be applied. The account includes interest on drawings, interest on capital, partnership salaries and the share of the residual profit or loss.

Income statements are exactly the same for partnerships as they are for a sole trader. The only difference comes after the profit for the year has been calculated. An **appropriation account** is now added on to show where the profit for the year is distributed, that is, how much profit or loss each partner receives and why. There are just four possible entries that may occur: interest on drawings, interest on capital, salaries and the share of any profits/losses each partner receives. You are making these adjustments from the point of view of the partnership as a whole and not for the individual partner. For example, interest on drawings reduces the individual partner's current account balance but increases the profit for the year for the partnership. This is a way of penalising a partner who is withdrawing significant amounts. If there is less cash in the partnership then an overdraft or loan may be needed, which would incur interest and hence reduce profits. The best source of finance for any business is from profit rather than external sources which have interest rates and arrangement fees attached.

A profit is credited to the partner's current account and a loss is debited to the partner's current account. You must ensure that you calculate interest on drawings and interest on capital separately for each partner and show them separately as in the illustration. You will either be given the interest on capital or interest on drawings figures or asked to calculate them using whatever percentage is given.

The examination question will normally tell you the profit sharing ratio. If it does not you should assume that the profits or losses are shared equally according to the Partnership Act 1890.

Illustration

Sharing profits

Harold, Moheber and Jane share their profits 3:2:1 respectively. This means that Harold receives the highest amount of profit. If the profit after adjusting for interest on drawings, interest on capital and salaries was £60,000 then divide £60,000 by 6 (3+2+1) and then multiply by 3 for Harold so £30,000, 2 for Moheber £20,000 and 1 for Jane £10,000. Add the individual partners' share of the profits together to check that they match the overall profit after appropriation.

Illustration

Appropriation account

Bonnie and Lucinda share their profits and losses equally as shown in the illustration of the current account. You can trace the entries from the current account onto the appropriation account.

Appropriation account for Bonnie and Lucinda for the year ended 31 March 2013

		£	£
Profit for the year			42,100
Add	Interest charged on drawings – Bonnie	800	
	– Lucinda	900	1,700
			43,800
Less	Salaries – Bonnie	15,000	
	– Lucinda	15,000	(30,000)
Less	Interest on capital – Bonnie	1,000	
	– Lucinda	800	(1,800)
			12,000
	Share of remaining profits		
	– Bonnie		6,000
	– Lucinda		6,000
			12,000

Fig. 3.3 *Appropriation account*

In this topic you will have learnt:

- how partners share their profits or losses
- the contents of a partnership agreement and the implications of the Partnership Act 1890 if there is no agreement
- the purpose and content of fixed capital and current accounts
- how to prepare a current account
- how to prepare an appropriation account.

Show the skills

Double-entry is an essential skill in order to successfully complete many aspects of partnership accounting and in particular the capital and current accounts. Re-visit double-entry from AS Unit 1 in order to prepare yourself. The whole process is much easier if you instinctively know whether to debit or credit the ledger account. The partners as individuals are essentially payables or liabilities of the partnership as the partnership owes the individual partners the money they have invested. If a partner has a closing balance on the credit side then the partnership owes the partner. If the closing balance is on the debit side then the partner owes the partnership which is not ideal as it indicates they have withdrawn money to which they were not entitled.

Practice questions

1   Explain why a successful sole trader may wish to enter into a partnership.

2   Sam and Jack are good friends but did not draw up a deed of partnership when they launched their gardening partnership. Outline the consequences of their decision.

3   George, Joseph and Stuart are in partnership together and have provided the following information for the year ended 31 December 2013:

	George £	Joseph £	Stuart £
Drawings	4,000	3,800	3,000
Interest on drawings	630	585	525
Capital	22,000	33,500	19,500
Partnership salaries	0	10,000	5,000
Opening balances of current accounts	600 credit	400 debit	350 debit
Share of residual profit	8,000	8,000	8,000

It should be noted that interest is allowed on partners' capitals at the rate of 6% per annum. (Interest on capital has been taken account of in calculating each partner's share of the residual profit.)

Prepare the partners' current accounts at 31 December 2013.

4   Mitesh, Sailesh and Kishen own a sports equipment shop. They share profits and losses in the ratios of 2:2:1 respectively and have provided you with the following information for the year ended 30 September 2013.

	Mitesh £	Sailesh £	Kishen £
Capital	78,000	42,000	95,500
Partnership salaries	10,000	0	15,000
Drawings	4,000	2,500	3,300

There is no interest on drawings. Interest on capital is to be allowed at 8% per annum.
The profit for the year was £62,800.

Prepare an appropriation account for the year ended 30 September 2013.

5   Jake and Sue are in partnership sharing profits and losses 3:1. The loss for the year ended 31 July 2013 was £6,200.

At 1 August 2012 the following balances appeared in the partners' accounts:

	Capital account	Current account
Jake	80,000	1,800
Sue	35,000	2,100

- There have been no changes to the capital accounts during the year; interest is allowed on their capital at the rate of 6% per annum.
- Sue is to be credited with a partnership salary of £9,000 per annum.
- Drawings for the year were Jake £12,200 and Sue £6,000 and interest is to be charged at 4% on each partner's total drawings.

(a)   Prepare an appropriation account for the year ending 31 July 2013.

(b)   Prepare the partners' current accounts to record the information given above.

(c)   Explain what is indicated by the closing balances on the partners' current accounts.

Topic 2   Preparing the financial statements of partnerships: more complex profit-sharing arrangements

In this topic you will learn how to:

- prepare end-of-year financial statements of partnerships

- prepare appropriation accounts and current accounts where profit sharing arrangements have changed during the course of the year.

Statement of financial position (balance sheet) of a partnership

The statement of financial position (balance sheet) of a partnership is very similar in many respects to one of a sole trader with sections for non-current assets, current assets, current liabilities and non-current liabilities. The difference comes at the end with the Financed by section, which shows where the capital has come from to fund the partnership. This is made up of both the fixed capital and the current accounts of all the partners. It is common practice to show the final capital account balance and then the breakdown of the current accounts. It is then clear how much each partner has invested or withdrawn from the partnership, how much profit they have received and so on. A debit balance on a current account is shown as a negative with brackets on a statement of financial position (balance sheet).

Illustration

A statement of financial position (balance sheet) extract for a partnership

Statement of financial position (balance sheet) (extract) for Neelum and Lloyd at 31 December 2013

	£	£	£
Financed by:			
Capital accounts			
Neelum		150,000	
Lloyd		225,000	
			375,000
Current accounts	Neelum	Lloyd	
Opening balance	2,200	(800)	
Add: salary	13,500	15,000	
Interest on capital	7,500	11,250	
Share of profit	20,000	20,000	
	43,200	45,450	
Less: drawings	25,300	40,000	
Interest on drawings	8,800	9,350	
	9,100	(3,900)	
			5,200
			380,200

Fig. 3.4 *Balance sheet extract for a partnership*

The closing balances on the current accounts are a credit for Neelum of £9,100 and a debit for Lloyd of £3,900. This means that Lloyd owes the partnership £3,900 and the partnership owes Neelum £9,100. Their closing balances are netted off to arrive at £5,200 which is then added to their closing capital accounts of £375,000 to show the balancing figure of £380,200.

Changes in partnership agreements

There will be times when a partner wishes to introduce more capital or withdraw some. It might be agreed that the current profit sharing ratio is not now a fair reflection of the amount of risk or work being undertaken by each partner and that it needs changing. The essential point to remember is to produce an appropriation account for the time period before the change and then another one for the following period. So, if a partner introduced capital six months into the financial year you would need to complete an appropriation account with the interest on capital for his original amount of capital and then another one for the second six months which has the interest calculated on the new amount of capital. Examination questions could involve one partner introducing more capital and the other withdrawing some so you essentially have four different amounts of interest on capital to calculate. Questions could also involve changes in the partners' profit sharing ratio to reflect any changes in working practices or investment positions.

Illustration

Example of a change in capital

Jeff, Simon and Beth are partners in the Pony Shack, which sells horse equipment. Their accounting period is for 12 months from 1 January. They have agreed that interest on capital is 5%. Jeff's capital balance was £200,000 throughout the year. Simon's capital balance was £200,000 until 1 July when he increased it to £340,000. Beth's capital balance was £300,000 until she reduced it by £116,000 on 1 July. The profit for the year was £68,000 and is accrued equally each month (same profit earned each month). They share profits and losses equally.

You need to calculate two separate interest on capital figures for both Simon and Beth as they have different amounts of capital during the year.

Simon has £200,000 × 5% = £10,000 then divide by 2 as it is for half a year = £5,000.

Then, £340,000 × 5% = £17,000 divide by 2 = £8,500.

Activity

6 Show how Beth's interest on capital has been calculated.

Appropriation account for Jeff, Simon and Beth for the year ended 31 December 2013

		£	£
Profit for the year			68,000
Less	Interest on capital – Jeff	10,000	
	– Simon	13,500	
	– Beth	12,100	
			35,600
			32,400
	Share of remaining profits		
	– Jeff		10,800
	–Simon		10,800
	– Beth		10,800
			32,400

Fig. 3.5 *Appropriation account showing a change in capital*

Illustration

Changes in a partnership agreement

The following appropriation account shows how a change of partnership agreement part way through the year should be shown. Originally the partners split the profits and losses equally, but on 1 June they decide to share profits 3:2 and to have interest on capital. It is assumed that the profit of £80,000 has accrued evenly throughout the year. The profit for the year for the first six months is £40,000. For the second six months the interest on capital is subtracted to leave £38,200. This is then shared between the partners by dividing £38,200 by 5 and then multiplying by 3 for Spencer, which is £22,920, and by 2 for Olivia, which is £15,280.

Study tip

Where the partnership agreement is changed during the year or the amounts of capital the partners have changes, ensure that you calculate interest on capital for the balances prior the change and then afterwards in order to find the amount for the year.

Appropriation account for Spencer and Olivia for the year ended 31 December 2013

		£	£
Profit for the year – first 6 months			40,000
Share of profits	– Spencer	20,000	
	– Olivia	20,000	
			40,000
Profit for the year – second 6 months			40,000
	Interest on capital		
Less	– Spencer	1,000	
	– Olivia	800	
			1,800
			38,200
	Share of remaining profits		
	– Spencer		22,920
	– Olivia		15,280
			38,200

Fig. 3.6 *Appropriation account showing a change in partnership agreement*

In this topic you will have learnt:

- how to complete a set of financial statements for a partnership
- how to prepare appropriation accounts and current accounts where there have been changes during the year such as profit sharing or capital balances.

Practice questions

1   Freya owns and runs a garden centre. She employs her son, Seb, who has a degree in horticulture and is keen to develop the online aspect of the business. Freya is considering offering Seb a partnership as he has recently inherited a large sum from his grandfather that could be used to expand the business.

Discuss whether or not Freya should enter into partnership with Seb.

2   Luke and Charlie are partners in a sauna installation business and have the following partnership agreement:
- partnership salaries are Luke £12,000 and Charlie £10,000 per annum
- interest on capital 10% per annum
- profits and losses to be shared equally.

Capital and current account balances at 31 May 2013

	Luke £	Charlie £
Capital account	48,000	20,000
Current account	3,500 credit	1,500 debit

The following information was available for the year ending 31 May 2013, after the preparation of the income statement:

	£
Drawings – Luke	12,000
Drawings – Charlie	14,000
Profit for the year	72,000
Property (premises) at cost	75,000
Vans at cost	32,000
Bank	8,100
Cash	2,500
Trade receivables	9,500
Trade payables	3,100
Provision for depreciation for vans	8,000

(a) Prepare an appropriation account for the year ended 31 May 2013.

(b) Prepare a statement of financial position (balance sheet) at 31 May 2013.

3   Lauren and Emmie are in partnership and start on 1 January 2012 with no partnership agreement. Lauren was then advised by her accountant to draw up a partnership agreement and on 1 July 2012 it was agreed that:

■ profits will be shared 2:1 respectively

■ interest on capital accounts will be 10% per annum

■ interest will be charged on drawings

■ profit for the year was £68,000 and it can be assumed that this accrued evenly throughout the year

■ partnership salaries will be introduced.

	Lauren £	Emmie £
Capital accounts 1 January 2012	30,000	20,000
Drawings for the year	14,200	12,750
Partnership salaries per annum	10,000	8,000
Interest on drawings for 1 July–31 December 2013	850	700

(a) Prepare the appropriation account for the year ended 31 December 2012.

(b) Prepare the partners' current accounts for the year ended 31 December 2012.

4   Stephen, James and Will are in partnership sharing profits and losses in the ratio 2:2:1 respectively. The partnership made a profit of £48,400 during the year ended 30 November 2013.

The following information is provided at 30 November 2013:

	Stephen £	James £	Will £
Capital accounts 1 December 2013	50,000	60,000	30,000
Current accounts 1 December 2013	600 credit	400 debit	1,000 credit
Drawings for the year	2,000	1,800	500
Partnership salaries	0	3,000	2,000

Interest is charged on drawings at a rate of 8% per annum on the full amount of each partner's drawings and interest allowed on capital of 6% per annum. The partners agreed that James should withdraw £10,000 from his capital and that Will should introduce the same amount on 1 June 2013.

(a)   Prepare the appropriation account for the year ended 30 November 2013.

(b)   Prepare the partners' capital and current accounts for the year ended 30 November 2013.

5   AQA ACC3 June 2012

Kelly and Roche are in partnership. They did not have a partnership agreement.

Roche made a loan to the partnership during the year ended 31 March 2011 and no repayments have been made.

From 1 August 2011, the partners decided to prepare a formal partnership agreement and the terms were as follows:

■   Interest on the partner's loan account is to be 4% per annum.

■   Interest on partners' capital accounts is to be 6% per annum.

■   Interest on partners' total drawings is to be charged at 3% per annum. (For the period 1 August 2011 to 31 March 2012, interest on drawings is: Kelly £592; Roche £472.)

■   Kelly's partnership salary is to be £15,900 per annum.

■   Profits and losses will be split between Kelly and Roche in the proportion 3:1 respectively.

No account has been taken of the interest on Roche's loan. The draft profit for the year ended 31 March 2012 was £41,400. Profits were accrued evenly before allowing for loan interest.

The following balances were extracted from the books of account for the year ended 31 March 2012.

	Kelly £	Roche £
Capital accounts	98,500	78,800
Drawings for the year	29,600	23,600
Current accounts at 1 April 2011	11,820	(9,456)
Partner's loan account		12,000

Prepare the partners' appropriation account for the year ended 31 March 2012, showing clearly the appropriation of profit for the periods:

■   1 April 2011–31 July 2011

■   1 August 2011–31 March 2012.

4 Partnership and changes in partners

Key term

Retirement of a partner: a structural change to the partnership and creates a 'new' partnership as a result. When a partner decides to retire we need to calculate the latest profit, the current worth of the partnership and perhaps reward the retiring partner for goodwill built up.

In this chapter we build on Chapter 3 and consider the accounting approaches needed in order to record the retirement and/or admission of a partner. We also look at what happens when a partnership is dissolved. The **retirement of a partner** could be followed by the admission of a new partner. When a partner retires we need to calculate how much the retiring partner is due to receive and how best this can be funded. If a new partner joins we need to ensure that our assets are appropriately valued. Goodwill needs to be considered in both situations. When a partnership comes to an end, the reality of having unlimited liability can become an issue with some partners having to cover the shortfall of others who may not have the required capital to cover their share of losses. It is important to take a logical approach to all types of partnership question and read carefully what the key changes are, make a note of the date when any changes occurred and then act accordingly.

Topic 1 Retirement of a partner

In this topic you will learn how to:

- calculate a revaluation surplus or deficit based on changes in asset values perhaps upon the retirement of a partner

- divide a revaluation surplus or deficit among the partners

- explain the term 'goodwill' and why it is not normally recorded in accounting records

- calculate the adjustment necessary to partners' capital balances as a result of valuing goodwill upon the retirement of a partner

- record the return of capital to a retiring partner by implementing various options including transfer of funds to a loan account, payment in cash or by the transfer of another asset

A limited company has its own separate legal entity and continues independently of its shareholders; with a partnership, when one partner dies or leaves a partnership then a new partnership is formed.

Case study

Walker, Scott and Cavendish

Walker, Scott and Cavendish are a successful partnership in Manchester who are estate agents dealing exclusively with the luxury end of the market. In addition to selling houses and apartments they also have a rental division that is particularly in demand from city workers who want the convenience of living in the city centre with all it has to offer. Cavendish has decided that he would now like to spend time with his family and would like to retire from the fast-paced life of property.

Stages needed when a partner retires

When a partner retires it is important to calculate how much their share of the partnership is worth. The other partners can then decide how best to finance this share. For example, the retiring partner could transfer the amount due to a loan account, a loan from the bank could be used, or the decision whether to bring a new partner in who can replace the retiring one and bring in capital themselves can be made.

1 We need to begin with the capital from the most recent statement of financial position (balance sheet).

2 Add to this any revaluation surplus or deduct deficit due to the partner.

■ prepare the statement of
financial position (balance
sheet) of the new partnership
after the retirement of a
partner

■ evaluate the options open to
a partnership in returning the
capital of a retiring partner.

3 Make **adjustments for goodwill**.

4 Add the latest current account balance if in credit or deduct if it
is a debit.

5 Decide how to pay the retiring partner the amount due.

Revaluation and intangible assets (goodwill)

These two processes are linked together as we will see in the following
illustration. The **revaluation account** records the change in value of
assets such as property (premises) or inventory. Property (premises) will
usually have increased in value whereas other assets such as inventory
may have fallen in value. Goodwill is essentially paid by the new partner
and existing partners receive the benefit in their capital accounts.
Eventually the new partner will recover this initial loss in his/her capital
account by receiving a share in future profits. Goodwill reflects the client
base or profit that has been built up over the partnership. It is only fair
to reward a retiring partner with their share of having established and
developed a successful partnership. Goodwill is intangible, which means
it has no physical substance and since it is largely based on reputation,
the popularity of the product or service it could be lost very quickly.
For this reason it is often considered good practice to write it off, in
other words remove it from the statement of financial position (balance
sheet). If goodwill is to remain on the books it appears as an asset on the
statement of financial position (balance sheet). You create goodwill in the
old partnership profit sharing ratio and write it off in the new partnership
profit sharing ratio.

Illustration

Retirement of a partner

Walker, Scott and Cavendish share profits and losses in the ratio 2:2:1.
They provide the following information:

**Statement of financial position (balance sheet) for Walker, Scott and Cavendish
at 30 April 2013**

	£	£
Non-current assets		85,000
Current assets	60,000	
Current liabilities	22,500	37,500
		122,500
Capital accounts – Walker		50,000
– Scott		25,000
– Cavendish		47,500
		122,500

Fig. 4.1 *Summary statement of financial position (balance sheet)*

Cavendish has decided to retire on 30 April 2013.

The partners have agreed that:

▪ non-current assets be valued at £100,000

▪ goodwill be valued at £40,000 and then be written off

▪ from 1 May 2013 profits and losses will be shared equally.

Firstly, we need to prepare a revaluation account:

Dr	Revaluation Account		Cr
Inventory	2,000	Non-current assets	15,000
Capital a/c – W	5,200		
– S	5,200		
– C	2,600		
	15,000		15,000

Fig. 4.2 *Revaluation account*

The non-current assets entry of £15,000 is how much the non-current assets have increased in value by. Inventory has fallen in value by £2,000. Perhaps it has deteriorated or is less popular now. £13,000 is then split between the partners in the old profit sharing ratio.

Dr	Goodwill Account		Cr
Capital – W	16,000	Capital – W	20,000
– S	16,000	– C	20,000
– C	8,000		
	40,000		40,000

Fig. 4.3 *Goodwill account*

To create the goodwill we debit the account in the old profit sharing ratios. To write off the goodwill account we split the amount between the remaining partners in the new profit sharing amount and credit the goodwill account.

We are now ready to enter these amounts in the capital accounts. As with current accounts it is much easier for both you and the examiner if you use the layout shown below rather than individual accounts for each partner.

Dr	Capital Account						Cr
	W	S	C		W	S	C
Goodwill	20,000	20,000	-	Bal b/d	50,000	25,000	47,500
Loan			58,100	Revaluation	5,200	5,200	2,600
Bal c/d	51,200	26,200		Goodwill	16,000	16,000	8,000
	71,200	46,200	58,100		71,200	46,200	58,100
				Bal b/d	51,200	26,200	

Fig. 4.4 *Capital accounts*

As you can see, instead of Cavendish having a closing capital account balance he has a loan, which is how much the partnership owes him for his share in the partnership. The remaining partners need to decide how best to deal with paying this amount to him.

Activity

1 Consider the advantages and disadvantages of the different ways in which Cavendish can be repaid his investment.

The new statement of financial position (balance sheet) will look like this:

Statement of financial position (balance sheet) for Walker and Scott at 30 April 2013

	£	£
Non-current assets		100,000
Current assets	58,000	
Current liabilities	22,500	35,500
		135,500
Capital accounts – Walker		51,200
– Scott		26,200
Loan – Cavendish		58,100
		135,500

Fig. 4.5 *Statement of financial position (balance sheet) after retirement*

How to settle liability owing to the retiring partner

There are several ways that this can be done:

1 Introduce a new partner and use the capital they introduce to pay off the retiring partner. If there will be a gap in skills, knowledge or finance, or too much work for the remaining partners then the admission of a new partner should be considered.

2 Bank overdraft. If a large enough overdraft can be secured this can be a flexible way of paying the partner as it can be easily repaid once enough cash is in the business, and finance costs (interest payable) are only charged on the amount outstanding. If the business knows it is soon to receive a substantial amount in revenue or income then this could be a good idea.

3 Bank loan. This could be used over a longer time period and if a large sum is needed. It will affect the monthly cash flow as usually finance costs (interest payable) and part of the capital will be repaid each month. Budgeting will be easier as the exact amount due each month is known.

4 Loan from retiring partner. This may have a cheaper interest rate than the loan or overdraft, but it could mean that the retiring partner still wishes to maintain some control and have a say over the partnership and its decisions.

In this topic you will have learnt:

- how to record the revaluation of tangible assets on the retirement of a partner

- why goodwill is not normally recorded in the accounting system and how an adjustment for goodwill should be made in the partners' capital accounts

- how to redraft the statement of financial position (balance sheet) immediately after the retirement of a partner

- how the remaining partners can discharge any liability to the retiring partner, and the benefits and drawbacks of the options.

Practice questions

1 Lewis, Eric and Katie are in partnership, sharing profits and losses in the ratio 3:2:1. They provide the following information:

Statement of financial position (balance sheet) for Lewis, Eric and Katie at 30 September 2013

	£	£
Non-current assets		120,000
Other current assets	36,000	
Bank	2,000	
Current liabilities	(22,000)	16,000
		136,000
Capital accounts – Lewis		82,000
– Eric		30,000
– Katie		24,000
		136,000

Eric has decided to retire on 30 September 2013.

The partners have agreed that:

- non-current assets be valued at £135,000
- current assets (excluding bank) to be valued at £33,000
- goodwill be valued at £48,000 and then be written off
- Lewis and Katie will continue in partnership, sharing profits and losses equally. The amount due to Eric will initially be placed in a loan account.

(a) Prepare the three partners' capital accounts at 30 September 2013, showing the effects of Eric's retirement.

(b) Prepare a statement of financial position (balance sheet) at 30 September 2013, following Eric's retirement.

2   Betsy, Lola and Ismail have been in partnership for five years sharing profits and losses in the ratio 2:2:1 respectively.

Statement of financial position (balance sheet) for Betsy, Lola and Ismail at 31 March 2013

	£	£
Non-current assets		110,000
Other current assets	28,000	
Bank	4,500	
Current liabilities	(18,000)	14,500
		124,500
Capital accounts – Betsy		53,000
– Lola		43,500
– Ismail		28,000
		124,500

Betsy has decided to leave and become a sole trader on 31 March 2013. The partners have agreed the following asset valuations to be applied.

	£
Non-current assets	230,000
Goodwill	50,000
Current assets (excluding bank)	26,000

Goodwill is not to appear in the books of account and in the short term the amount owed to Betsy should be transferred to a loan account. Lola and Ismail have agreed to share profits and losses equally after Betsy has left the partnership.

(a)   Prepare the three partners' capital accounts at 31 March 2013, showing the effects of Betsy's departure.

(b)   Prepare a statement of financial position (balance sheet) at 31 March 2013, showing the effects of Betsy's departure.

(c)   Advise Lola and Ismail how the debt owed to Betsy could be settled.

3   Nathan, Joe and Sana are in partnership sharing profits and losses in the ratio 2:2:1 respectively. Nathan decides to retire on 31 December 2012 when the partnership statement of financial position (balance sheet) is as follows:

Statement of financial position (balance sheet) for Nathan, Joe and Sana at 31 December 2012

	£
Net assets	200,000
Capital accounts	
– Nathan	50,000
– Joe	72,000
– Sana	78,000
	200,000

Goodwill is agreed at a valuation of £36,000 and will not remain in the books. Joe and Sana are to continue in partnership and will share profits and losses in the ratio 2:1 respectively. Nathan agrees to leave £20,000 of the amount due to him as a loan to the new partnership. The balance of the amount due to Nathan will be paid in cash.

(a)   Prepare the three partners' capital accounts at 31 December 2012, showing the effects of Nathan's retirement.

(b)   Prepare a statement of financial position (balance sheet) at 31 December 2012, showing the effects of Nathan's retirement.

Topic 2   Admission of a partner

In this topic you will learn how to:

■ calculate and share a revaluation of assets prior to the admission of a partner

■ calculate and make entries for a goodwill adjustment in the capital accounts of the partners

■ record the capital introduced by an incoming partner

■ record entries to alter the relative balances of partners' capital accounts where individual partners pay in, or take out, funds

■ prepare the statement of financial position (balance sheet) after the admission of the new partner.

In this topic we will be examining the accounting entries needed for the admission of a partner. We may need a new partner because an existing one has retired, left or because we require additional capital. It could also be that we have a gap in our skills or knowledge and require the expertise of a new partner. Whatever the reason it is essential that we consider the goodwill that has already been built up in the current partnership, revalue the tangible assets and reward the existing partners accordingly.

■ Revaluation

If a revaluation takes place which increases the value of the asset, which is usually the case with property (premises), then we:

■ **Debit** revaluation account

■ **Credit** each partner in their profit sharing ratio prior to the new partner.

If the asset has fallen in value, as could be the case with inventory, then we should:

■ **Debit** each partner in their profit sharing ratio prior to the new partner

■ **Credit** revaluation account.

Admitting a new partner and revaluation

Walker and Scott have decided to admit Rahman into their partnership as they have found it difficult to cope since the retirement of Cavendish. They currently share profits and losses equally. At 31 December 2013, their assets had the following values:

	£
Non-current assets	
Property (premises)	200,000
Fixtures and fittings	64,000
Motor vehicles	36,000
	300,000

Fig. 4.6 *Non-current assets*

Rahman is admitted as a partner on 1 January 2014 when the assets were revalued as follows:

	£
Non-current assets	
Property (premises)	300,000
Fixtures and fittings	50,000
Motor vehicles	24,000
	374,000

Fig. 4.7 *Revaluation of assets*

Dr		Revaluation Account		Cr
	£			£
Fixtures and fittings	14,000	Property (premises)		100,000
Motor vehicles	12,000			
Capital – Walker	37,000			
Capital – Scott	37,000			
	100,000			100,000

Fig. 4.8 *Revalued non-current assets*

Walker and Scott's capital accounts will both be credited with £37,000 to reflect the overall increase in assets of £74,000, which is the increase in property (premises) of £100,000 less the fall in value of the fixtures and fittings and motor vehicles of £26,000.

Treatment of goodwill

Goodwill is an intangible asset that is often calculated to reflect the success so far of the partnership when a partner joins or leaves the partnership. It is considered good accounting practice to write off goodwill immediately as shown here:

1 Not to remain in books

The first stage is as above:

- **Debit** goodwill account
- **Credit** existing partners' capital accounts in old profit sharing ratio.

We then need to remove the goodwill:

- **Debit** all partners' capital accounts in new profit sharing ratio
- **Credit** goodwill account.

To create goodwill we credit in old ratio and to destroy (write off) goodwill we debit in the new ratio.

2 To remain in books

- **Debit** goodwill account
- **Credit** existing partners' capital accounts in old profit sharing ratio.

If goodwill remains then it is shown on the statement of financial position (balance sheet) in the non-current assets section.

■ Illustration

Admitting a new partner and goodwill

Brian and Chris are partners in a firm and share profits equally. Their capital account balances are £75,000 and £50,000 respectively. On 1 January 2013 they admit Jerry as a partner when the profit or loss sharing ratio will be 2:2:1 respectively. Goodwill is valued at £15,000 and is to be written off. Jerry paid £45,000 into the firm's bank account and brings in a van worth £5,000 as capital.

Table 1 *Share of goodwill*

	First stage Old partner sharing Create goodwill = credit	Second stage New partner sharing Destroy goodwill = debit
Brian	$\frac{1}{2}$ = £7,500	$\frac{2}{5}$ = £6,000
Chris	$\frac{1}{2}$ = £7,500	$\frac{2}{5}$ = £6,000
Jerry	-	$\frac{1}{5}$ = £3,000

We can now enter these amounts into the capital accounts.

Dr	Capital Account						Cr
	B	C	J		B	C	J
Goodwill	6,000	6,000	3,000	Bal b/d	75,000	50,000	
				Bank			45,000
				Van			5,000
Bal c/d	76,500	51,500	47,000	Goodwill	7,500	7,500	
	82,500	57,500	50,000		82,500	57,500	50,000
				Bal b/d	76,500	51,500	47,000

Fig. 4.9 *Capital accounts*

The money and van that Jerry introduces will be debited to the bank and van accounts and credited to the capital account. The overall effect of Jerry joining the partnership is that Brian and Chris now have increased capital account balances and Jerry's balance is less than the amount he has contributed. He has in effect, bought his way into the partnership.

	£	£
Capital accounts – Brian		76,500
– Chris		51,500
– Jerry		47,000
		175,000

Fig. 4.10 *Statement of financial position (balance sheet) extract to show new capital account balances*

Changes needed in the financial statements to reflect the introduction of a new partner

As we saw in the previous topic, if there is a change to the partnership agreement about sharing profits or losses or interest on capital etc. during the year, the appropriation account needs splitting into two sections to show this. In the same way, if a new partner is introduced during the year then we need to draw up an appropriation account prior to the new partner joining and then for the period after they have joined. On the statement of financial position (balance sheet) we must adjust for any cash or non-current assets they have introduced and also show their new capital account balance, which may well be less than they introduced if goodwill was introduced and then written off.

In this topic you will have learnt:

- why a new partner may be introduced and the need to ensure existing partners are suitably rewarded for their previous efforts
- how to make adjustments for goodwill
- how to record the capital introduced by the new partner
- how to appropriate profits in a year when a new partner has been introduced part way through
- how to redraft a partnership statement of financial position (balance sheet) immediately after the admission of a partner.

Activity

2 In pairs, discuss the potential advantages and disadvantages to admitting a new partner into a partnership that has been in existence for 10 years.

Practice questions

1.   Bella and Fizz are partners and have shared profits and losses equally. Their capital account balances on 31 December 2012 were: Bella £82,000 and Fizz £63,000. On 1 January 2013 they admitted Jake as a partner who contributed as capital £38,000 in cash and machinery worth £26,000. The new profit/loss sharing ratio for Bella, Fizz and Jake was agreed to be 3:2:1 respectively. Goodwill was to be valued at £18,000 and was not to remain in the books of account.

   Prepare capital accounts showing the effects of Jake joining the partnership.

2.   Jones and Tuthill share profits 2:1 respectively. They admit Brown as a partner on 1 July 2013, who will contribute £40,000 cash as capital.

Statement of financial position (balance sheet) for Jones and Tuthill at 30 June 2013

	£	£
Non-current assets		
Property (premises)		170,000
Motor vehicles		85,000
Current assets		
Inventory	12,000	
Bank	3,500	
		15,500
		270,500
Capital accounts		
– Jones		150,000
– Tuthill		120,500
		270,500

The partners decide to revalue their assets as follows:

	£
Property (premises)	220,000
Motor vehicles	70,000
Inventory	10,000
Goodwill	12,000

The new profit sharing ratio for Jones, Tuthill and Brown will be 2:2:1 respectively. Goodwill is not to remain in the accounts.

  (a)   Prepare capital accounts for the three partners showing the effects of the revaluation and Brown's admission as a partner.

  (b)   Prepare the statement of financial position (balance sheet) for the partnership at 1 July 2013.

3   Petra and Enid are in partnership, sharing profits and losses 2:1 respectively.

The partnership statement of financial position (balance sheet) at 30 April 2013 was as follows:

Petra and Enid Statement of financial position (balance sheet) at 30 April 2013

	£	£
Non-current assets		320,000
Current assets		
Inventory	22,500	
Trade receivables	10,800	
	33,300	
Current liabilities		
Bank overdraft	15,820	
Trade payables	8,880	
	24,700	
Net current assets		8,600
		328,600
Capital accounts		
– Petra	180,000	
– Enid	140,000	320,000
Current accounts		
– Petra	11,860	
– Enid	(3,260)	8,600
		328,600

The partners have agreed that the following should take effect on 1 May 2013:

- Beradin is to be introduced as a new partner with a capital investment of £120,000 paid into the bank.
- The profit sharing ratio for Petra, Enid and Beradin is to be 3:2:1 respectively.
- Non-current assets are to be revalued at £410,000.
- Goodwill is to be valued at £60,000 and this will not be maintained in the books of account.
- Enid should have a credit balance of £9,000 on her current account. A transfer from her capital account is needed to achieve this.
- Petra will transfer £30,000 from her capital account to a loan account.

(a)   Prepare the partnership capital accounts for the three partners after the above effects have taken place.

(b)   Re-draft the statement of financial position (balance sheet) to show the changes made following Beradin's admission as a partner.

(c)   Evaluate the decision to keep separate capital and current accounts.

Topic 3   Dissolution of a partnership

Key terms

Dissolution: this takes place when a partnership ceases to continue operating. It could be because the partners want this to happen or are forced to because of problems such as lack of cash and/or profit.

Realisation account: used to close the partnership and calculate the profit or loss for the partners once all the assets have been sold or taken over.

▪ Reasons for dissolution

Unlike a limited company, which can continue in existence regardless of changes in ownership, if anything happens to one of the partners of a partnership then that partnership is dissolved, ceases to exist, and a new one emerges if that is what the remaining partners desire. It could be that a partner wishes to set up independently, is declared bankrupt, dies or wishes to retire.

It is important that the partnership uses its assets to cover any debts in the order of: trade payables, partners' loan accounts and then finally, if there is money remaining, this will go to the partners' capital accounts. Some of the partners may wish to take over assets themselves, alternatively assets may be sold for cash or taken over by another business.

Stages in dissolution

In order to carry out the process of **dissolution** we need to use a **realisation account**:

Table 2 *Contents of a realisation account*

Debit	Credit
The net book value of the assets to be sold (non-current and current assets)	Proceeds from the sale of the assets
Discounts allowed	Discounts received
Costs of the dissolution	Loss on realisation
Profit on realisation	

When customers and suppliers hear that the partnership is being dissolved then they may in the customers' case not be so willing to pay in full and in the suppliers' case be willing to receive less than originally owed. The discounts allowed are calculated by starting with the trade receivables figure and then subtracting what is actually received from them. The discounts received amount are the trade payables from the statement of financial position (balance sheet) less what the business actually pays them. There will either be a profit or loss on realisation, not both.

Follow these eight stages below:

1 Enter opening balances of the ledger accounts, for example capital accounts, realisation and bank accounts, you have been asked to produce.

2 Enter the non-current asset values and current assets excluding trade receivables. Do not include the bank balance on the debit of realisation account.

3 Debit bank account with what is actually received from trade receivables (not necessarily what they owed) and credit bank with what the business pays trade payables.

4 Calculate discounts received and discounts allowed and enter in realisation account.

5   Receive cash for assets sold, debit bank and credit realisation account.

6   If a partner takes over assets then debit their capital account and credit realisation account with the value of the asset.

7   Close down realisation account and post the balances on the realisation account in the partners' capital accounts.

8   Close down capital account and bank account.

Illustration

Dissolution of a partnership

Martha and Jamie have decided to sell their partnership to Heather for £80,000. They had no partnership agreement. The trade receivables pay them £8,000 and trade payables are paid £5,000. Costs of the dissolution are £1,800, for example accountant's and solicitor's fees. Their latest summarised statement of financial position (balance sheet) is below.

Statement of financial position (balance sheet) for Martha and Jamie at 30 September

	£	£
Non-current assets		40,000
Current assets		
Inventory	22,000	
Trade receivables	10,000	
Bank	2,000	
	34,000	
Current liabilities		
Trade payables	6,000	
Net current assets		28,000
		68,000
Capital accounts – Martha		38,000
– Jamie		30,000
		68,000

Fig. 4.11 *Summarised statement of financial position (balance sheet)*

Dr		Realisation Account		Cr
Non-current assets	40,000	Discounts received	1,000
Inventory	22,000	Bank – Heather	80,000
Discounts allowed	2,000		
Costs of dissolution	1,800		
Capital – Martha	7,600		
Capital – Jamie	7,600		
	81,000		81,000

Fig. 4.12 *Realisation account*

The discounts are calculated by finding the difference between what they were owed and owing and the actual payments which then took place. The profit on dissolution is £15,200 which is split equally between the two partners since they had no partnership agreement. If they did have a partnership agreement, it would have been split according to the profit sharing ratio.

Dr			Capital Account		Cr
	M	J		M	J
Bank	45,600	37,600	Bal b/d	38,000	30,000
			Profit on realisation	7,600	7,600
	45,600	37,600		45,600	37,600

Fig. 4.13 *Capital account*

The profit from realisation has been entered in each partner's capital account and balancing these accounts off will provide us with the amount each partner is entitled to take from the bank account to finally close down the partnership.

Dr		Bank Account	Cr
Bal b/d	2,000	Trade payables	5,000
Trade receivables	8,000	Costs of dissolution	1,800
Capital – Heather	80,000	Capital – Martha	45,600
		Capital – Jamie	37,600
	90,000		90,000

Fig. 4.14 *Bank account*

We can tell that we have completed the process correctly because our bank account has no closing balance. The owners of any business are the last to be repaid.

Transfer of assets to partners

A partner may decide to take over some of the assets, perhaps because they want to set up as a sole trader or start a new partnership. If this happens then we:

- **Credit** the realisation account with the agreed value of the asset taken over
- **Debit** the partners' capital accounts with the agreed value of the asset taken over.

Sale of assets to a company

It is possible that a company may wish to take over some of the assets. They could provide cash, ordinary shares or debentures in return. It is important to note that it is what the ordinary shares are *worth* currently that we need to record and not how much their face value is.

Illustration

Company purchasing partnership

Dylan Ltd agrees to a purchase consideration of £250,000 being made up of: £50,000 cash, £65,000 6% debentures and 25,000 ordinary shares of £1 each. We can set up an account for Dylan Ltd that will show us how much the shares are currently worth.

Dr		Dylan Ltd Account		Cr
	£			£
Realisation	250,000	Bank		50,000
		Debentures		65,000
		Ordinary shares		135,000
	250,000			250,000

Fig. 4.15 *Account for Dylan Ltd*

This means that the ordinary shares are currently worth
$$\frac{£135,000}{25,000} = £5.40 \text{ each.}$$

Unless otherwise stated the purchase consideration in terms of shares and debentures from a company is split amongst the partners in the profit sharing ratio. The entries will be on the debit side of the capital accounts and the credit side of the purchasing company account if one has been set up. Any cash received from the company is debited to the bank account.

Activity

3 How much are the shares worth each if Stalyvegas Ltd offer a purchase consideration of £300,000 being made up of £70,000 cash, £57,000 5% debentures and 30,000 ordinary shares of £2 each?

Garner v. Murray

If, after joining the current account balances with the capital accounts, and after transfer of profit or loss on realisation to capital accounts, a capital account ends up with a debit balance, this means that the partner concerned owes money and that there is a **capital deficiency**. The partner will need to use his or her personal cash to cover this debit balance, but what if he or she does not have enough cash to do this? The ***Garner v. Murray*** case ruled that this shortfall must be covered by the other partners in proportion to their last agreed capital account ratio. Therefore, the partner who had most capital invested according to the most recent statement of financial position (balance sheet) must take on the largest share of the shortfall.

Illustration

Sharing a shortfall

James has a debit balance on his capital account of £600. His partners Fran and Tim must share this according to their last statement of financial position (balance sheet) capital account balances. Fran had £9,000 and Tim had £6,000 for their capital accounts, which means 3:2. So, £600 needs sharing, with Fran contributing £360 $\left(\frac{600}{5} \times 3\right)$ and Tim £240 $\left(\frac{600}{5} \times 2\right)$.

Dr				Capital Account			Cr
	£	£	£		£	£	£
	J	F	T		J	F	T
Bal b/d	600			Bal b/d		9,000	6,000
Capital – James		360	240	Capital – Fran	360		
Bank		8,640	5,760	Capital – Tim	240		
	600	9,000	6,000		600	9,000	6,000

Fig. 4.16 *Capital account*

Instead of calculating the balances carried down, the balancing figures represent the amount Fran and Tim will withdraw from the bank account.

Study tip

As with previous partnership questions it is essential to show detailed workings, for example when adjusting to deal with a partner's debit balance on their capital account after dissolution.

In this topic you will have learnt:

- the reasons why partnerships dissolve
- how to record the realisation of assets and the discharge of liabilities
- how to record assets taken over by a partner
- the preparation of a realisation account to show the profit/loss on realisation and its distribution among partners
- the preparation of capital accounts showing entries arising during the realisation process and the final discharge of any liability to a partner
- how to deal with a deficiency on a partner's capital account using *Garner v. Murray*.

Mossley Ltd agrees to take over all of the non-current assets, except for the delivery vans at a valuation of £100,000. They will pay £70,000 cash, and also issue to the partners 20,000 ordinary shares of £1 each. Ruth and Sasha each took over a delivery van at an agreed valuation of £4,000 for each van. Inventory was sold for £5,000 and trade receivables paid £8,000. Trade payables were paid £4,000 and the costs of dissolution were £1,500.

Prepare the realisation account, the partners' capital accounts and the bank account following dissolution.

4   Anton, Bert and Clara have been in partnership and share profits and losses in the ratio 2:2:1 respectively. The demand for their service has declined and they have agreed to dissolve the partnership on 31 March 2013.

Anton, Bert and Clara Statement of financial position (balance sheet) at 31 March 2013

	£	£
All assets other than bank		187,000
Bank	1,800	
Current liabilities		
Trade payables	52,000	
Net current liabilities		(50,200)
		136,800
Capital accounts		
– Anton	79,800	
– Bert	53,200	
– Clara	2,000	135,000
Current accounts		
– Anton	1,000	
– Bert	2,800	
– Clara	(2,000)	1,800
		136,800

Samuel agreed to purchase the business for £120,000 cash. All assets and liabilities other than the bank balance were taken over by Samuel. The dissolution took place and was completed on 1 April 2013. Clara was bankrupt and unable to repay any potential liability due to the partnership from personal funds.

Prepare the realisation account, capital accounts for the three partners and bank account to record the dissolution at 1 April 2013.

5 Published accounts of limited companies

![icons]

In this chapter you will learn how to:

- identify the main elements of published reports

- explain why companies publish their accounts

- demonstrate a knowledge of corporate report requirements of different user groups

- explain the limitations of published accounts

- prepare a schedule of non-current assets

- explain the duties of directors and auditors with regard to the accounts.

Key terms

IAS 1 Presentation of Financial Statements: sets out overall requirements for the presentation of financial statements.

Non-current assets: the term used for assets that are expensive items bought not primarily to resell but to help generate profits and keep for longer than one financial year, for example property (premises) and machinery.

Companies Act 1985, amended 1989 and 2006: this Act governs limited companies and requires that limited companies prepare and publish accounts annually. In 1989 EU directives (rules imposed by the European Union to harmonise accounting) were added.

Potential investors: are people who may wish to buy shares in a company. The element of risk and potential reward is important to this group and also whether they intend to invest for the short or long term.

You have already been introduced to this topic during the AS in Unit 2. Limited companies are required by law to produce financial statements and to adhere to the requirements of **IAS 1 Presentation of Financial Statements**. Many companies have their financial statements on their website, which means anyone can examine them. They can appear not to provide as much detail compared to a sole trader or partnership, but this is because notes accompany the accounts which then give more detail, for example a schedule of **non-current assets** that shows the non-current assets bought and sold during the year and depreciation involved. The published accounts are not used for day-to-day decision making within the actual business as they are a summary and the internal accounts will provide far more detail. You need to know the different user groups of the accounts and the limitations as well as possible uses for those groups. Directors have duties to perform in the process as do the auditors who are appointed by the shareholders to check the accounts produced. You do not need to be able to compile the published accounts but you need to have a good understanding of their content, purpose and who has responsibilities concerning them.

Purpose of published accounts

Published accounts are regulated by the **Companies Act 1985, amended 1989 and 2006** and IAS 1 Presentation of Financial Statements. Copies of published accounts must be sent to each shareholder and debenture holder. It is increasingly easy to access published accounts on company websites so they are firmly in the public domain. Annual returns must be completed and filed with the Registrar and kept at Companies House in Cardiff. In addition to the legal requirement, published accounts are used by shareholders and **potential investors** to allow them to make decisions, for example whether to continue investing. A benefit of becoming a limited company is having limited liability. This means that unlike a sole trader or partnership, shareholders only lose the amount of money they have invested in shares, but not their personal assets. The ability to raise far larger amounts of finance is also an advantage, but there are legal obligations that come with the status:

- Financial statements must be audited (checked by a qualified accountant) to ensure a 'true and fair view'. This is not cheap and involves showing your financial statements to outsiders for scrutiny. It also depends on the size of the company; smaller companies are no longer required to have an audit carried out.

- Financial statements must be completed and filed with the Registrar of Companies.

Users of published accounts

Table 1 *Possible users of published accounts*

User	Reason
Investors, potential investors	To decide whether to buy or sell shares, dividend payout, assess risk (e.g. shares can lose as well as gain value and dividend payments are not guaranteed so investment could be safer elsewhere)
Pressure groups such as Greenpeace	For social accounting purposes, for example, how much pollution is the company creating, their carbon footprint, etc.
Competitors	For benchmarking performance
Banks and financial institutions	So that lending risk can be assessed
Analysts	To make recommendations based on current and historic information
Trade payables (suppliers)	To check on the company's liquidity and make trading decisions such as how long a credit period to give or how much credit to extend
Employees	To see how profitable the business is to assess whether their jobs are safe and if they can ask for higher wages

Key terms

Analysts: their job is to closely examine trends, published accounts and the **Stock Exchange** where stocks and shares are bought and sold, and make predictions.

Stock Exchange: this is where stocks and shares are bought and sold, mainly second-hand shares and government securities.

Show the skills

Being able to understand published financial statements is an essential skill if you wish to enter a career in accountancy. Often the first area trainee accountants work in is audit, which involves checking for a true and fair view. Auditors cannot physically check every single transaction of a business so they use a sampling system in order to gain an overall sense of the correctness of the financial statements.

Link

The role of the International Accounting Standards Board will be examined in more depth in Chapter 7.

Limitations of published accounts

Whilst published accounts are widely available their actual value can be limited for the following reasons:

1 They are based on historical information and the figures may not reflect the current trading position, the economic situation such as low inflation or high interest rates. Published accounts take a long time to be produced and as soon as they are published they are already several months out of date. Past performance is no guarantee of future performance.

2 Summarised figures hide the detail such as exactly how much is spent on advertising or on staff wages. This means it is hard to perform specific benchmarking. It would be very useful for a competitor to know exactly how much the company spends on their call centre in the Far East, but this information is hidden under the umbrella of administration expenses so is impossible to know.

3 Window dressing occurs, which is legal but means that a certain amount of massaging of figures may take place which presents the company in the best possible light. For example, a revaluation of property (premises) may have recently taken place to boost the non-current assets on the statement of financial position (balance sheet).

4 The human aspect such as labour turnover, absenteeism rates, is not included which can tell the user a lot about the morale and qualities such as qualifications and experience of the workforce that cannot be seen by the published accounts alone.

5 Not accessible/too complex for non-specialist users. Think back to when you first started studying accounting. Many of the terms are unfamiliar and also have several ways of being expressed, for example sales, turnover, income and revenue.

Case study

Sunny Dreams plc is a newly established public limited company. The two brothers who previously started their luxury holiday business as a partnership and then a private limited company understand they will now have to publish their accounts in accordance with IAS 1 Presentation of Financial Statements. They had become familiar with partnership financial statements and internal limited company accounts and are now faced with income statements, statements of cash flows and statements of financial position (balance sheets), which all look different.

Contents of published accounts

The contents are decided by the International Accounting Standards Board whose job it is to ensure that accounting standards help produce high-quality, transparent and comparable accounts. For now we will concentrate on IAS 1 Presentation of Financial Statements, which states that a set of financial statements contains:

- an income statement
- a statement of financial position (balance sheet)
- a **statement of changes in equity** for the period (this deals with any share issues, dividend paid, etc.)
- a statement of cash flows for the period (covered by IAS 7)
- notes, comprising a summary of significant accounting policies and other explanatory information
- **directors'** report
- **auditors'** report.

A company can also publish any other information it chooses, for example a chairman's report.

Illustration

Income statements

Income statement for Sunny Dreams plc for the year ended 31 December 2012

	£000
Revenue	1,000
Cost of sales	(400)
Gross profit	600
Distribution costs	(25)
Administration expenses	(30)
Profit from operations	545
Finance income	8
Finance cost	(13)
Profit before tax	540
Taxation	(150)
Profit for the year	390

Fig. 5.1 *Income statement for Sunny Dreams plc*

Most of these terms should be familiar to you but here is a reminder:

- Revenue = sales, turnover less any sales returns/returns inwards.
- Cost of sales = opening inventory plus purchases and carriage inwards less purchase returns/returns outwards less closing inventory.
- Gross profit = revenue less cost of sales.
- Distribution costs = costs involved in storing, packing and delivering goods to customers.
- Administration expenses = management and all other expenses such as advertising. Discounts allowed should be added to this category and discounts received subtracted.
- Profit from operations = gross profit less distribution costs and administration expenses.
- Finance income = interest received from any investment property (investments) the company may have.
- Finance cost = the cost of interest on loans, debentures, preference share dividends or overdrafts.
- Profit before tax = this is used to calculate the amount of corporation tax the company needs to pay.
- Taxation = this cannot be known until the income statement is produced so also appears on the statement of financial position (balance sheet) as a current liability.
- Profit for the year = this is available to be distributed to shareholders or to be retained in the company.

Illustration

Statement of financial position (balance sheet)

Statement of financial position (balance sheet) for Sunny Dreams plc at 31 December 2012

	2012	2011
	£000	£000
Non-current assets		
Property, plant and equipment	120,000	78,000
Current assets		
Inventories	5,000	4,850
Trade and other receivables (prepayments)	250	225
Cash and cash equivalents (bank and cash)	10	13
	5,260	5,088
Total assets	125,260	83,088
EQUITY		
Share capital	70,000	60,000
Share premium account	5,000	3,000
Revaluation account	4,500	2,500
Retained earnings	5,559	5,269

(Continued)

Key terms

Inventories: raw materials, work in progress or finished goods.

Trade and other receivables (prepayments): this includes trade receivables and other receivables (prepayments), amounts owed to the business or that the business have paid for in advance, e.g. rent and insurance.

Cash and cash equivalents (bank and cash): cash held in the business and/or in the bank account.

Total equity	85,059	70,769
Non-current liabilities		
Mortgage	20,000	0
Debenture loan 6%	10,000	10,000
	30,000	10,000
Current liabilities		
Trade and other payables (accruals)	10,051	2,219
Tax payable	150	100
Total current liabilities	10,201	2,319
Total liabilities	40,201	12,319
Total equity and liabilities	125,260	83,088

Fig. 5.2 *Statement of financial position (balance sheet)*

Illustration

Statement of changes in equity

You should be familiar with the statement of changes in equity from AS Unit 2.

Statement of changes in equity for Sunny Dreams plc for the year ended 31 December 2012

	Share capital £000	Share premium £000	Revaluation reserve £000	Retained earnings £000	Total £000
At 1 January 2012	60,000	3,000	2,500	5,269	70,769
Issue of shares	10,000	2,000			12,000
Revaluation			2,000		2,000
Profit for the year				390	390
Equity dividends paid				(100)	(100)
At 31 December 2012	70,000	5,000	4,500	5,559	85,059

Fig. 5.3 *Statement of changes in equity*

The statement of changes in equity links figures shown on the income statement and on the statement of financial position (balance sheet). Profit for the year is taken from the income statement. Only dividends actually paid now appear in the financial statements. The opening and closing balances on the statement of changes in equity reflect the equity section of the statement of financial position (balance sheet) at the start and end of the year. In the illustration Sunny Dreams plc have issued shares above their nominal value as both the share capital and the share premium accounts have increased. There has also been an upward revaluation of property (premises).

Terminology

You will already be familiar with the terminology in examinations that have been in existence since January 2013. There are other IAS terms that may be used in future examinations.

Table 2 *Previous UK and international terms*

Previous UK term	International term
Accruals	Other payables
Balance sheet	Statement of financial position
Bank and cash	Cash and cash equivalents
Interest payable	Finance costs
Interest receivable	Investment revenues
Investments	Investment property
Land and buildings	Property
Prepayments	Other receivables
Sundry expenses	Other operating expenses
Sundry incomes	Other operating incomes

Show the skills

Not all company directors come from a financial background so an important skill you need to develop is how to interpret and present your findings in a user friendly manner. If you assume the user only has a limited grasp of accounting you should be able to explain the main elements such as profitability, liquidity and the overall well-being of the business. You should be able to recommend areas for improvement and how these improvements could be brought about, for example high amounts of receivables could mean there is a need for tighter credit control.

■ Duties of directors and auditors

The directors are responsible for the whole process of completing the financial statements. They approve and sign the financial statements and ensure they are filed with the Registrar of Companies. The directors have a responsibility of stewardship to record accurate information in the published financial statements. The financial statements need to be comparable, understandable, relevant and reliable. The directors also need to ensure the financial statements are audited. The directors must ensure that sufficient detail is supplied whilst maintaining confidentiality to protect the company from its competitors.

Auditors are independent of the company and act in an unbiased manner to check that the declared financial information and company position is accurately reported. The role of the auditor is to form an opinion and declare whether a true and fair view is provided. 'True and fair' follows the principle that accounting records should be based on facts or a reasonable estimate of the company's financial position. Auditors are entitled to any information they require to enable them to form an opinion. They will never state that the financial statements are 100% accurate because they can only check the information provided by the company. The true and fair opinion is based on the fact that the accounts contain estimates and are subject to a number of decisions. All auditors' reports state the same information and include:

■ respective responsibilities of directors and auditors

■ basis of audit opinion

■ opinion.

However, auditors will also state if they feel the company has not complied with financial reporting regulations at any point in their accounts.

If you look at different companies' auditors' reports you will see how similar they all are. Directors' reports on the other hand do vary as they are specifically reporting on the company involved. The report will look at the achievements of the past year, profits and dividends, the board of directors, employee involvement, equal opportunities to name just a few. They also give notice of when the **annual general meeting (AGM)** will be held where shareholders get the chance to voice their opinions.

Schedule of non-current assets

A **schedule of non-current assets** is a summary of the non-current assets and any new non-current assets bought (additions), sold (disposals), revaluations (usually property (premises)) and the depreciation attached to the disposals and the depreciation charge for the year. This allows us to calculate the net book value which then appears on the statement of financial position (balance sheet).

■ Illustration

Schedule of non-current assets

Schedule of non-current assets for Triangle Nuts plc at 31 March 2013

	Property (premises) £000	Fixtures, fittings and equipment £000
Cost at 1 April 2012	2,000	625
Revaluation	100	
Additions		130
Disposals		(100)
Cost at 31 March 2013	2,100	655
Depreciation at 1 April 2012	20	300
Disposals		(28)
Revaluation	(20)	
Charge for year	15	55
Depreciation at 31 March 2012	15	327
Net book value at 1 April 2012	1,980	325
Net book value at 31 March 2013	2,085	328

Fig. 5.4 *Schedule of non-current assets*

- Cost at start = the original cost of the non-current assets before depreciation is applied.
- Revaluation = how much the non-current asset is increasing in value. The double entry is to debit property (premises) and credit revaluation reserve.
- Additions = any non-current assets bought throughout the year, at cost.
- Disposals = any non-current assets that have been sold during the year, at cost.
- Cost at end = the cost of the non-current assets after any additions, disposals or revaluation taking place.
- Depreciation at start = the accumulated depreciation so far.

Study tip

A common examination question is to be asked the difference between the reports of the auditors and the directors and the different criteria these two reports fulfil. You must ensure you are familiar with the reason for and role of the auditor in reporting on published accounts.

Key terms

Annual general meeting (AGM): the yearly meeting of a limited company to which all the shareholders are invited.

Schedule of non-current assets: this records the movement/revaluation (purchase and sale) of non-current assets and the depreciation attached to the movements.

4   The following data was taken from the accounting records of Blue Monkey plc for the year ended 31 December 2012:

	Non-current assets at 1 January 2012	Depreciation at 1 January 2012	Non-current assets bought during 2012
Property (premises)	700,000	-	-
Motor vehicles	120,000	35,000	22,000
Office equipment	80,000	12,000	38,000

Motor vehicles are depreciated at 15% reducing balance method and office equipment at 5% straight line on cost. A full year's depreciation is provided in the year of purchase, but none in the year of sale.

A motor vehicle bought in April 2008 was sold in June 2012 for £15,000. The original cost of the motor vehicle was £52,000.

During August 2012 office equipment, with an original cost of £12,500 and with a written down value of £6,200, was sold at a loss of £2,000.

On 2 February 2012 property (premises) was revalued at £850,000.

(a)   Prepare the schedule of non-current assets for Blue Monkey plc for the year ended 31 December 2012.

(b)   Explain the purpose of a schedule of non-current assets and one benefit to a particular user group.

5   AQA ACC3 June 2012

The directors of Chalfont plc have provided the following extract from the statement of financial position (balance sheet) at 31 May 2011.

	Cost	Depreciation	NBV
	£	£	£
Property (premises), plant and equipment			
Plant and machinery	175,000	56,750	118,250

During the year ended 31 May 2012, the following transactions took place:

(1)   A machine that originally cost £34,500 was sold on 31 December 2011. This machine had originally been purchased on 1 October 2009.

(2)   A new machine was purchased for £49,500 on 1 January 2012.

The following is an extract from the company's statement of accounting policies:

■ Plant and machinery is depreciated using the straight-line method at 20% per annum.

■ All non-current assets are depreciated on a month-by-month basis.

Prepare the schedule of non-current assets for the year ended 31 May 2012.

6   Statement of cash flows

In this chapter you will learn how to:

- prepare a statement of cash flows (using the indirect method following the format given in IAS 7)

- explain the value of statements of cash flows to potential user groups

- analyse or access the information contained within a statement of cash flows.

Key terms

Statement of cash flows: shows how cash has been generated (cash inflows) and how it has been spent (cash outflows), information not provided by the income statement or statement of financial position (balance sheet).

IAS 7 Statement of Cash Flows: the International Accounting Standard we need to follow using the indirect method. It provides information about changes in cash and cash equivalents (bank and cash).

Indirect method: profit or loss is adjusted to determine operating cash flow.

Operating activities: revenue-producing activities that are not investing or financing.

A major cause of misunderstanding for non-specialists is how a company can have a profit of, say, £2m but then also have a bank overdraft of £25,000. There are several reasons for this, for example the application of the other payables (accruals) concept, purchase of non-current assets and repayment of loans. The company may yet have to receive cash owed to them from trade receivables. They may have used cash to buy non-current assets that only affect the profit through depreciation spread over the assets' life even though a large sum of cash may have been retained to pay for the assets immediately. Income statements show what should have happened rather than the physical movement of cash. Profit is the difference between revenues and costs incurred in the financial year, which does not necessarily match the actual amounts paid and received. **Statements of cash flows** link the operating profit a company has made with its cash and cash equivalents (bank and cash) position. Cash equivalents are short-term, highly liquid investment property (investments) that are readily convertible to a known amount of cash. **IAS 7 Statement of Cash Flows** enables companies to report their cash generation and absorption in a way that helps provide information to users who need to make decisions based on the financial statements. Do not confuse a statement of cash flows with a cash flow forecast (cash budget). Statements of cash flows show what has happened while cash flow forecasts show what is forecast to happen. Essentially the statement of cash flows provides the link from the profit or loss on the income statement through to the cash and cash equivalents (bank and cash) on the statement of financial position (balance sheet). This process is carried out in three stages which we will now examine.

Calculation of profit from operations

You will be familiar with this process as essentially you are working backwards (using the **indirect method**) to recreate the profit from operations that you have covered in Chapter 5. The first step is to find the company's profit from operations for that year. This is not part of the statement of cash flows itself but is needed to form the basis of calculating the company's net cash position from its normal **operating activities**.

Illustration

How to calculate profit from operations

	£000
Profit for the year	203
Taxation	20
Finance cost	8
Finance income	(3)
Profit from operations	228

Fig. 6.1 *Calculation of profit from operations*

2 Gain on disposal of non-current assets	(66)
3 Decrease in inventory	130
4 Increase in trade receivables	(47)
5 Increase in trade payables	223
Cash from operations	724
6 Interest paid	(4)
7 Taxation paid	(60)
Net cash from operating activities	660

Fig. 6.8 *Reconciliation of operating profit to net cash flow*

The numbers in the above table are explained below so that you can follow the process.

The profit from operations of £319,000 was calculated in the previous section and this is the starting point.

Adjustments are then made which have the effect of either increasing or decreasing the cash in the business.

1   Depreciation for the year is found in the schedule of non-current assets and is £165,000. This needs adding back as it is a book-entry and is not an actual movement of cash.

	£000
Cost	665
Depreciation to date	(65)
NBV	600
Proceeds	666
Profit on disposal	66

Fig. 6.9 *Calculation of profit on disposal*

2   The cost in the above calculation represents the disposal of non-current assets at cost, that is, what was paid for them initially. The depreciation for those non-current assets then needs to be subtracted as otherwise the depreciation includes charges for non-current assets that are no longer owned. This leaves the net book value, which should then be compared with the proceeds of the sale to obtain the profit or loss on disposal. If the non-current asset is sold for more than its net book value there is a profit as shown here, and if it is sold for less there is a loss. This is a book entry and has to be subtracted from the loss of operations. The physical movement of cash takes place when the assets are bought and sold. The proceeds of £666,000 will appear in the actual statement of cash flows.

3   The decrease in inventory is added because it means an increase in cash in the business as the inventory amount has fallen so has been converted into cash.

4   The increase in trade receivables means that more cash is owed to Move It plc so this movement must be subtracted.

5   The increase in trade payables means that Move It plc owes more cash so this is added because more cash is being retained in the company.

6 The taxation paid represents what was owed in 2011 accounts so is the amount that has now actually been paid, so it is subtracted since it will have decreased the cash.

7 The net cash from operating activities is the amount left after the adjustments. If it had been negative it would be called the net cash used in operating activities. This figure is now taken onto the statement of cash flows in the third and final section.

The statement of cash flows

Move It plc statement of cash flows for the year ended 31 December 2012

	£000	£000
Net cash from operating activities		660
Cash flows from investing activities		
Purchase of non-current assets	(2,396)	
Proceeds from sale of non-current assets	666	
Net cash used in investing activities		(1,730)
Cash flows from financing activities		
Proceeds of issue of equity share capital	1,600	
Repayment of long-term borrowings	(200)	
Dividends paid	(175)	
Net cash from financing activities		1,225
Net increase in cash and cash equivalents (bank and cash)		155
Cash and cash equivalents (bank and cash) at the beginning of the year		(143)
Cash and cash equivalents (bank and cash) at the end of the year		12

Fig. 6.10 *Move It plc statement of cash flows*

The net cash from operating activities was calculated in the above section.

The purchase of non-current assets is shown at cost and is the same amount as additions from the schedule of non-current assets.

The proceeds from sales of non-current assets is the cash received from the sale of non-current assets and not the profit.

The net cash used in investing activities is the amount spent on non-current assets, which is a negative figure as it represents a fall in cash plus any proceeds from the sale of non-current assets.

The next section examines financing activities, any shares bought or sold, dividends paid and loans or debentures taken or repaid. In the above case, Move It plc have increased their share capital by £1,600,000. This is found by subtracting 2011 share capital from 2012, £5,680,000 − £4,410,000 = £1,270,000 and then adding this to the increase in share premium. Remember, share premium is the additional amount that a share is sold for above its nominal or face value. In this case, £771,000 −£441,000 = £330,000. Add the two together, £1,270,000 + £330,000 = £1,600,000.

The dividends paid are what have physically been paid and is taken from the statement of changes in equity. Proposed dividends no longer appear in the financial statements.

The net increase in cash and cash equivalents (bank and cash) can be compared to the movement on the statement of financial position (balance sheet), which was £143,000 negative (cash and cash equivalents (bank and cash) of £32,000 and bank overdraft £175,000) in 2011 and increasing to £12,000 (cash and cash equivalents (bank and cash) of £112,000 and bank overdraft £100,000) in 2012, a positive movement of £155,000 overall.

Value to users of statement of cash flows

The movement to using IAS 7 to prepare statements of cash flows has simplified the process into three sections: operating, investing and financing. There is considerable flexibility as to which sections cash flows are allocated provided there is year-on-year consistency. Statements of cash flows can be a better indicator of liquidity than the other financial statements since they clearly show the **cash inflows** and **cash outflows**. There may well be some valid reasons why a company has a negative movement of cash. They may be expanding so purchasing larger amounts of non-current assets than they normally would. The statement of cash flows hopefully enables the user to examine how efficiently cash resources have been used that year. It can also be used to compare different companies that are of similar nature. A potential investor who is looking for a safe investment may value a healthy cash position as an indicator that the company can afford to pay dividends on a regular basis. Other investors may be looking for a longer commitment and be pleased to see considerable investment in non-current assets that will yield considerable profits and hopefully dividends in the future. Statements of cash flows are more objective than the income statement as they examine the true cash flow movements rather than what should have happened. An income statement includes revenue and book adjustments that may never be paid so is more subjective than the actual cash position.

Uses of a statement of cash flows

1 Shows how a business has generated cash inflows.
2 Shows how a business has used cash resources during the year.
3 Inter-business comparisons can be made.
4 Highlights liquidity problems so that action can be taken such as securing an overdraft.
5 Shows movements in ordinary share capital and debentures.
6 Shows sources of internal funding and how reliant on external funding the company is.
7 Enables shareholders to see if the directors have used cash and resources sensibly.

In this chapter you will have learnt:

- how to prepare a statement of cash flows using the indirect method following IAS 7
- how to explain the value of statements of cash flows to potential user groups
- how to comment on statements of cash flows by examining the three separate stages.

Key terms

Cash inflows: movements of cash into the company such as a share issue or sale of non-current assets.

Cash outflows: movements of cash out of the company, for example repaying loans or purchasing non-current assets.

Link

In AS Unit 2 you will have learnt about gearing. This ratio looks at how heavily a company rely on external financing. This is relevant for statements of cash flows as a user may be concerned about increases in external borrowings due to the interest needing to be paid. It is important to consider what the company is using the borrowings for as if it is to expand the business, for example building a new factory, this could eventually improve profits.

Study tip

Read carefully what you are required to answer in the examination. You may need to calculate profit from operations or the net cash from operating activities or a full statement of cash flows.

Practice questions

1   Explain how a company can make a loss but still have an increase in cash and cash equivalents (bank and cash).

2   Discuss the extent to which cash is more significant for business survival than profit.

3   Calculate the operating profit or loss from the following information for the year ended 31 March 2013:

Retained earnings at 31 March 2013	£125,000
Retained earnings at 31 March 2012	£45,000
Taxation for the year ended 31 March 2013	£32,000
Interest paid for the year ended 31 March 2013	£4,000

4   The following information has been extracted from the published accounts of Bump on Board plc for the year ended 31 December 2012.

	£000
Operating profit	32,874
Depreciation	3,890
Increase in trade inventories	20
Decrease in trade receivables	8
Increase in payables	4
Profit on disposal of property (premises), plant and equipment	2

Prepare the reconciliation of operating profit to net cash flow from operating activities for the year ended 31 December 2012.

5   AQA ACC3 January 2012
The following information is available for Hinault plc.

	Year ended 31 October 2011 £	Year ended 31 October 2010 £
5% debenture loan	60,000	40,000
Inventories	14,600	17,200
Non-current assets NBV	75,900	92,400
Tax liability	31,500	29,200
Trade payables	12,560	9,040
Trade receivables	15,700	11,300

Additional information for the year ended 31 October 2011.
(i)   A non-current asset with a net book value of £3,600 was sold for £2,800 during the year.
(ii)   A £20,000 debenture loan was issued on 1 May 2011.
(iii) All debenture loan interest was paid during the year.
(iv)   Profit for the year was £105,000.

(v) Tax on profit for the year was £32,960.

(vi) There were no purchases of non-current assets during the year.

Prepare an extract from the statement of cash flows for Hinault plc for the year ended 31 October 2011 showing net cash (used in)/from operating activities. The extract should be prepared in accordance with IAS 7.

6 The statements of financial position (balance sheets) of Fuchsia Magic plc at 30 September 2013 are shown below.

Statements of financial position (balance sheets) for Fuchsia Magic plc at 30 September 2013

	2013		2012	
	£000	£000	£000	£000
ASSETS				
Non-current assets (note 1)		400		350
Current assets				
Inventories	200		134	
Trade and other receivables (prepayments)	180		150	
Cash and cash equivalents (bank and cash)	0		30	
		380		314
Total assets		780		664
EQUITY				
Ordinary share capital		375		350
Share premium account		50		45
Retained earnings (note 2)		82		72
Total equity		507		467
Non-current liabilities				
Debentures		50		43
Current liabilities				
Bank overdraft	10		0	
Trade and other payables (accruals)	198		143	
Tax liabilities	15		11	
		223		154
Total liabilities		273		197
Total liabilities and equity		780		664

Note 1 – There were no disposals of non-current assets and the depreciation for the year ended 30 September 2013 was £8,000.

Note 2 – An extract from the income statement for the year ended 30 September 2013 is as follows:

	£
Profit from operations	33,000
Finance costs (interest payable)	(4,000)
Profit before taxation	29,000
Taxation	(16,000)
Profit for the year	13,000

Dividends paid in 2013 were £3,000.

Prepare a statement of cash flows in accordance with IAS 7 for the year ended 30 September 2013.

7   The finance director of Turbot plc is preparing the company's statement of cash flows for the year ended 30 September 2013. The accountant provides the following details:

	£000
Decrease in inventories	48
Tax paid	182
Increase in trade receivables	33
Increase in trade payables	84
Interest expense	221
Proceeds of share issue	400
Loss before tax	650

Cash and cash equivalents (bank and cash)

	£000
At 1 October 2012	53
At 30 September 2013	36

Schedule of non-current assets for the year ended 30 September 2013

	£000
Cost	
At 1 October 2012	16,320
Additions	945
Disposals	(451)
At 30 September 2013	16,814
Depreciation	
At 1 October 2012	7,308
Charge for the year	1,212
Disposals	(402)
At 30 September 2013	8,118
Net book value	
At 1 October 2012	9,012
At 30 September 2013	8,696

The proceeds from the sale of non-current assets in the year ended 30 September 2013 was £59,000. Prepare a statement of cash flows for the year ended 30 September 2013, in accordance with IAS 7.

7 International Accounting Standards

In this chapter you will learn how to:

■ explain the purposes of international accounting standards

■ apply the main points of the standards you need to know

■ apply each of the standards to particular situations described for a limited company.

Key term

Accounting standard: this allows financial statements to be compiled in a format that allows them to be compared over years and between companies.

Study tip

You must learn the number and title of each of the standards but you do not need to know the standards word for word. You should have a good understanding of the key features and be able to match them to scenarios given using appropriate accounting technology.

Detailed knowledge of each standard is not required.

Accounting standards were introduced to bring comparability of success between companies and to produce financial statements that minimised creative accounting and promoted consistency. Creative accounting involves companies showing their financial statements in the best possible light. This could be to attract potential investors or to avoid paying taxation. It is important this practice is minimised with the use of accounting standards in order to allow sufficient comparability of financial statements between years and companies. There are two main areas of creative accounting:

1 manipulation of profit, showing profit as being on an upward trend and so good quality

2 manipulation of liabilities, which involves the under-reporting of liabilities also known as off statement of financial position finance.

As soon as one 'loophole' (way to be creative with financial statements) has been dealt with then companies will find another way, so to deal with this modern accounting standards are based on principles rather than rules. The International Accounting Standards Board (IASB) uses a framework that deals with:

■ the objective of financial statements, to provide information about the financial position, performance and changes that are useful to users

■ qualities that financial information should have for it to be useful

■ definitions of the elements in financial statements (assets, liabilities, equity, income and expenses) and their recognition and measurement.

Activity

1 A good way of learning something new is to teach it to someone else! Split the standards between the members of your group and each research a standard. Produce a Microsoft PowerPoint presentation or an interesting handout that summarises the key points of the standards and present them to each other. You should then have a complete set of notes.

Case study

Music Now Ltd is a successful download music store that was previously a partnership between two friends, Wade and Trixy. Their accountant has advised them that their new status brings with it a considerable amount of standards to comply with. Wade and Trixy are confused about IASs and why they should bother to adhere to them. Their accountant assures them that it is essential to follow the IASs and he will ensure that they are explained to them so that they can make the best decisions in the interest of the newly formed limited company.

Purpose and importance of international accounting standards

All listed companies (not just the ones on the London Stock Exchange) in the EU have to now prepare their financial statements following the **International Accounting Standards**. Each of the standards will be taken in turn and the key points explained. IAS 1 Presentation of Financial Statements and IAS 7 Statement of Cash Flows are covered in Chapters 5 and 6 so will not be revisited here. Standards should enable financial statements to provide information that is useful in making economic decisions. The purpose of accounting standards is to address:

- Comparability – information provided for one period must be comparable with that provided for the previous period and between companies.
- Consistency – in order to achieve comparability, information must be given consistently from one period to another, and accounting policies must be fully disclosed.
- Understandability – users of financial statements are expected to have a reasonable knowledge of business and economic activities and accounting. This does not mean that a vital piece of information should be omitted just because it is complex.
- Relevant and reliable – there should not be major errors or any bias.

IAS 2 Inventories

Inventory is important as it is shown as an asset on the statement of financial position (balance sheet) and has a direct impact on the measurement of profit. Inventory can include:

- raw materials – materials to be used in production
- work in progress – goods in the process of production
- finished goods – goods held for sale.

Prudence is an important concept with inventory as we must value inventory at the lower of cost (what was paid for it) or net realisable value (selling price minus costs involved in repairing inventory into a saleable condition).

Case study

Inventory valuation

Music Now Ltd are considering changing their inventory valuation method from FIFO to AVCO.

IAS 1 refers to the presentation of financial statements. It states that there must be compliance with accounting concepts, including consistency, and therefore the same inventory valuation method should be used for all accounting periods. If there has been a material change in the way the business conducts its business, a change in methods is allowed, but such a change must be openly declared in the notes of the financial statements to bring the change to the attention of any user group.

Damaged goods for resale have been included in the inventory valuation at an original cost of £25,000. These goods will be sold at £32,000 but will need to be repaired at an additional cost of £12,000.

Key terms

International Accounting Standard: standards set by the International Accounting Standards Board.

IAS 2 Inventories: concerned with inventory as an asset and expense and how it is valued.

Show the skills

The skill of being able to apply a set of rules to a scenario is exactly what accountants must do every day. In order for financial statements to be comparable accountants must deal with situations according to the International Accounting Standards. This process does get easier with experience but there are frequently changes made in order to prevent accountants from exploiting loopholes.

The net realisable value = £32,000 − £12,000 = £20,000 which is £5,000 lower than the cost of £25,000. As the NRV is lower than cost then £5,000 would be deducted from inventories in current assets and also deducted from retained earnings.

The cost of inventories comprises all:

■ costs of purchases
■ 'other costs' incurred in bringing the inventories to their present location and condition
■ costs of conversion.

Take care with carriage: carriage inwards can be included in the cost of inventories but carriage outwards cannot. Remember, carriage inwards is the cost of goods coming into the business; carriage outwards is the cost of delivering goods to customers.

Inventories can be valued on the first in first out (FIFO) basis or using a weighted average method (AVCO). Inventory valuation will be examined in Chapter 8.

IAS 8 Accounting Policies, Changes in Accounting Estimates and Errors

IAS 8 addresses the criteria for selecting and changing accounting policies, together with the accounting treatments for changes in accounting policy and the correction of errors. The underlying issue here is that the information must be relevant and reliable.

Table 1 *Definitions needed for IAS 8*

Accounting policies	Prior period errors
Specific principles, bases, conventions, rules and practices applied by an entity in preparing and presenting financial statements.	The errors must be ones that were reasonably identifiable when the financial statements were authorised for issue.

Accounting policies must be applied consistently to similar events and transactions. Errors can arise from mistakes or misinterpretations. They must be corrected in the first set of financial statements issued after the discovery. Prior period errors must be restated as if the error has never happened. So, if you find an error with your inventory valuation you must go back and change the incorrect figure and follow this through to the latest set of financial statements. It should look as if the new policy or correction has always been there.

Accounting principles are the broad concepts that are applied in the preparation of accounting standards outlined in IAS 1, for example prudence, other payables (accruals), consistency, etc.

Accounting bases are methods used by directors in the preparation of the accounting statements. They identify acceptable methods and are intended to reduce subjectivity, for example the use of historic cost or revaluation as the method used to value assets.

Link

It is worth reminding yourself of the accounting concepts that you studied as part of AS Unit 2 as they play a considerable role in accounting standards.

Key term

IAS 8 Accounting Policies, Changes in Accounting Estimates and Errors: criteria for selecting and changing accounting policies.

■ Case study

Inventory valuation oversight

Music Now Ltd discovered that when the inventory valuation took place an area of the warehouse had not been checked. This amounted to £5,500 of inventory. When this was discovered the financial statements were corrected under IAS 8 to reflect the true situation at the time of the inventory valuation.

Examples of changes in accounting policies:

1 asset measurement changed from depreciated historic cost to revaluation

2 expenses reclassified from cost of sales to administrative

3 legislation changes

4 a new accounting standard leads to change.

It is important to look at a company's choice of accounting policies when performing ratio analysis and interpreting financial statements.

IAS 10 Events After the Reporting Period

IAS 10 explains the duties of companies and directors in looking for and adjusting for events after the reporting period. Companies have six months to file their accounts, which can be a long time in the business world, and major changes such as a fire that destroy the business buildings or a legal challenge resulting from prior transactions but only now brought to court can occur.

If material events exist at the statement of financial position (balance sheet) date and if the outcome is known before the accounts have been approved then the impact can be adjusted in the financial statements. An event is material if it would significantly impact on decisions and on the view of user groups, for example shareholders.

■ Illustration

Adjusting event

A credit customer who owed £22,000 at the year ended 31 March 2013 was declared bankrupt on 5 April 2013, before the financial statements had been approved by the board of directors.

This impact can be adjusted in the financial statements and £22,000 would be deducted from trade receivables in current assets and also deducted from retained earnings.

If there is evidence of conditions that existed at the statement of financial position (balance sheet) date then the accounts must be adjusted to reflect this.

If the amount(s) involved are material, then the amounts shown in the financial statements should be changed.

Examples could include:

■ a liability that existed at the year end, the value of which became clear after the statement of financial position (balance sheet) date

■ where a customer has become insolvent after the statement of financial position (balance sheet) date and the large debt is included in the year end trade receivables.

■ Key term

IAS 10 Events After the Reporting Period: these events may affect users' interpretation of the financial statements.

Show the skills

Shareholders need assurance that their investment is being handled to ensure long-term success of the company so that dividends are likely to be paid and share prices remain strong. By using International Accounting Standards the accountants are following guidelines that are used across the world. By learning the standards and key scenarios you are gaining a crucial skill for a career in accountancy that is transferable across the global business world.

Non-adjusting events are conditions that arise after the statement of financial position (balance sheet) date. They should be disclosed in the notes.

Case study

Non-adjusting event

Music Now Ltd has a financial year end of 31 December 2012. On 22 January 2013 there was a flood that damaged some computers and caused disruption.

The flood happened after the year end date and so would be classified as a non-adjusting event even though the financial statements may not have been approved by the board of directors. No adjustment is therefore made to the financial statements for the year end. However, if the impact of the event is deemed material then the event details will be disclosed in the notes to the financial statements.

If such events are material then they are disclosed by way of notes to the accounts. These notes would explain the nature of the event and if possible the likely financial consequences of the event.

Examples might include:

- a major restructuring of the business
- significant business commitments entered into after the statement of financial position (balance sheet) date.

For example, dividends declared after the statement of financial position (balance sheet) date are not recognised as a liability at the statement of financial position (balance sheet) date as they were not owing at that date so, no adjustment is made for them. Financial statements are usually prepared on the basis that the entity will continue as a going concern. If a decision to liquidate the entity or part of the entity or to cease trading is made after the statement of financial position (balance sheet) date, the going concern basis is no longer appropriate.

When events occur after the reporting period but before the date that the financial statements are authorised we need to know how best to handle them. We need to consider whether we have just been made aware of a condition that actually existed at the reporting period, in which case we do adjust, or if it arose after the reporting period there should be a disclosure in the notes. No changes can be made once the financial statements have been authorised.

IAS 16 Property, Plant and Equipment

Property, plant and equipment are recorded initially at cost, which includes all expenditure to get the item ready for use. They are often a major item of expenditure for a company so need to be accounted for carefully to avoid producing misleading financial statements. Expenditure on repairs and maintenance is classified as revenue expenditure and appears on the income statement. After it has been bought a company may choose to value the property, plant and equipment either at cost less accumulated depreciation, or at fair value (amount for which an asset could be sold less costs incurred to secure the sale) due to a revaluation. Property, plant and equipment are depreciated (cost shared) over their expected useful life. The depreciation amount takes into account any

Activity

2 Decide whether to adjust or not following IAS 10 for the scenarios below that occurred after the statement of financial position (balance sheet) date:

a a branch of the business was sold

b inventory included on the statement of financial position (balance sheet) was sold below cost

c major change in currency exchange rates.

Key term

IAS 16 Property, Plant and Equipment: this concerns tangible assets held for more than one accounting period and used in the production and supply of goods or services, or for administration.

expected residual amount. The method and rate are reviewed annually but should not be altered unless there is a good reason, due to the consistency concept which allows comparison of financial statements with previous years. Freehold land is not depreciated as land is a scarce commodity and unless discovered to be unusable due to environmental issues for example, it will generally increase in value. When an item of property, plant and equipment is disposed of, the profit or loss on disposal is included in the income statement.

Key information required:

- depreciation methods used (in our case, straight-line or reducing balance)
- useful economic lives or the depreciation rates used
- where material, the effect of a change of depreciation rate or method
- the cost or revalued amount of the assets
- the cumulative depreciation at the start and end of the financial year
- a reconciliation of the movements of property, plant and equipment.

■ Illustration

Valuing property, plant and equipment after restoration

A piece of equipment that had cost £70,000 several years ago has recently had a major overhaul costing £20,000. The equipment has a written down value of £40,000. The supervisor has declared the equipment to be as good as new and the directors have included the asset on the statement of financial position (balance sheet) at £60,000.

According to IAS 16 this is acceptable because the work has restored the economic benefits of the equipment and therefore reflects the revalued amount.

IAS 18 Revenue

IAS 18 is concerned with revenue from sale of goods, rendering of services and from the use by others of the company assets yielding interest, royalties and dividends. Usually revenue is recognised when it is likely that the economic benefits from the transaction will occur and can be measured. The realisation concept is behind this IAS, which involves income only being recognised when it is certain.

■ Key term

IAS 18 Revenue: includes revenue from sale of goods, rendering of services and use by others of entity assets yielding interest, royalties and dividends.

Table 2 *Revenue and when it is recognised*

Revenue	Recognised
Sale of goods revenue	when significant risks and rewards have been transferred to the buyer; when the seller has no control over the goods and goods or services have been exchanged
Rendering of services	percentage of completion method or, the extent of expenses that are recoverable, a recognisable proportion of an agreed service has already taken place normally in long-term contract situations

(Continued)

Interest	over time, on the effective yield on the product
Royalties	in accordance with the agreement
Dividends	when the shareholder has the right to receive payment

Timing is an important issue here, for example sales with delayed delivery, subscriptions for products, or fees for services delivered in parts over time. This is where window dressing or creative accounting can occur in order to boost sales and hence profits. IAS 18 states that, if there is uncertainty about the possibility of return, revenue is recognised when the goods or services have been delivered and the period of time for rejection has expired.

Case study

Music Now Ltd have decided to introduce a subscriptions service, which means that new material can be downloaded before it is released on CD in the stores. When the customer has used this service once then the period of time for rejection has expired and the profit can be recognised.

IAS 36 Impairment of Assets

Key term

IAS 36 Impairment of Assets: an asset must not be shown at more than the highest amount to be recovered through its use or sale.

An asset must not be carried in the financial statements at more than the highest amount to be recovered through its use or sale. If that is the case the asset is impaired and the company must reduce the carrying amount (the value of a non-current asset as shown in a statement of financial position (balance sheet) after the deduction of accumulated depreciation and accumulated impairment losses) of the asset to its recoverable amount (the higher of a non-current asset's fair value and its value in use) and recognise an impairment loss, which is like an extra depreciation expense. Fair value is the amount for which a non-current asset could be sold less any costs incurred in the sale. Value in use is calculated by discounting the future cash flows generated by the use of a non-current asset.

What could cause impairment?

- Decline in an asset's market value
- Adverse changes in the technological market or economic or legal environment
- Increase in market interest rates
- Obsolescence or damage of an asset
- Plans to discontinue or restructure operations
- Asset under performance compared with expected return

Goodwill and intangible assets with indefinite lives should be tested annually for impairment. The impairment losses should be charged to the income statement as an expense, unless the asset had previously been revalued upwards. If a revaluation has taken place then this must be removed. Sometimes a group of assets is considered rather than one and this is known as a cash-generating unit.

IAS 37 Provisions, Contingent Liabilities and Contingent Assets

A provision is an amount set aside out of profits for a known expense that is uncertain such as taxation. A liability is an existing obligation to make a payment due to a past event such as a loan.

Contingencies are concerned with possible events that may or may not happen, but which the concept of prudence means the company should take into account.

A contingent liability is a possible obligation that arises from past events whose outcome is based on uncertain future events or an obligation that is not recognised because it is not probable, or cannot be measured reliably.

A contingent asset is a possible asset that arises from past events and whose existence will only be confirmed by uncertain future events not wholly within the control of the company. It would not be prudent to recognise income that may never be realised.

Table 3 *Requirements of contingent assets and liabilities*

Likely/unlikely to occur	Liability of uncertain timing or amount	Asset of uncertain timing or amount
Virtually certain (therefore not contingent)	Make provision	Recognise (receivable)
Probable	Make provision	Disclose by note (contingent asset)
Possible	Disclose by note (contingent liability)	No disclosure
Remote	No disclosure	No disclosure

This IAS was introduced in response to creative accounting and originally it was felt that there was no need to have a standard concerning provisions. The measurement of a provision requires judgement about the amount, timing and risks of the cash flows required to settle the obligation. Care is needed when making judgements under conditions of uncertainty. Note how the prudence concept favours provisions for liabilities not assets.

IAS 38 Intangible Assets

An intangible asset is one without physical substance. Intangible assets are either purchased or internally generated. Only purchased intangible assets can be recognised in the financial statements as they have an established, real, provable market value. Internally generated goodwill or brand names cannot be recognised as the values are subjective. Intangible assets are shown in the financial statements in the same way that non-current assets are. Goodwill is the most common one but other examples include:

■ computer software
■ licences

- trademarks
- patents
- films
- copyrights
- import quotas.

A purchased intangible asset such as a patent is recognised in the financial statements at cost price. It is capitalised in the statement of financial position (balance sheet) if this cost can be reliably measured and if there are probable future economic benefits. An intangible asset with a predicted useful life is amortised (written off in a similar way to depreciation) using the straight-line method, and one with an indefinite life is tested annually for impairment (loss of value) and only then is the cost reduced.

The cost of generating an intangible asset internally is often difficult to distinguish from the cost of maintaining or improving the company's operations or goodwill. So, internally generated brands and customer lists are not intangible assets.

Research expenditure is an expense, and development expenditure needs to meet certain criteria to be an intangible asset. Development costs are the application of research and can either be shown in the income statement as an expense or capitalised as an intangible asset if they satisfy certain criteria such as being feasible.

Background information

In 1998 Rank Hovis McDougall decided to put a range of internally developed brand names onto the statement of financial position (balance sheet) at a figure of £678m. This became a new trend for companies, which IAS 38 has now put a stop to!

■ Illustration

Treatment of development costs

A product is due to be launched next year and the accountant is unsure of how to treat the development costs.

IAS 38 states that as the product is feasible the development costs can be capitalised as an intangible asset on the statement of financial position (balance sheet).

In this chapter you will have learnt:

- the purpose of accounting standards
- the key points of each of the IASs you need to know
- how to apply the standards to scenarios that a company may find itself in.

Practice questions

1　Explain the purpose and importance of accounting standards.

2　A company has spent £3m establishing a brand name. The managing director wishes to include this on the next statement of financial position (balance sheet) and to amortise it. Is this the appropriate treatment? Explain.

3　Hook Up have installed a new computer system at a cost of £3.5m. The finance director believes that the installation and training costs of £1m can also be included on the statement of financial position (balance sheet). Is she correct?

4　AQA ACC3 January 2011

The directors of Cole-Daniel plc are unsure about the correct accounting treatment of the following items in the financial statements for the year ended 31 October 2010.

(1)　Damaged finished goods for resale have been included in the inventory valuation at an original cost of £52,000. These goods will be sold at the original cost plus 20%. However, before sale, the inventory will need to be repaired at an additional cost of £12,500.

(2)　£62,000 has been spent on the purchase of a patent.

(3)　A credit customer who owed £35,000 at the year ended 31 October 2010 was declared bankrupt on 9 November 2010, before the financial statements had been approved by the Board of Directors.

(a)　Identify the accounting standard to be applied to each of the items (1) to (3).

(b)　Explain, with reference to the relevant accounting standard, how each of the items (1) to (3) should be treated in the financial statements.

5　Zesty Ltd has machinery with a carrying amount of £160,000. It has an estimated fair value of £95,000 and an estimated value in use of £115,000. The accountant is unsure how to value the machinery and has asked for your advice.

6　The legal team of Burgers Are Us Ltd has warned that a customer is suing the company for an estimated £30,000 as a result of horse meat being found in the company's products. The case will be concluded after this financial year and it is probable that Burgers Are Us Ltd will lose. Advise the finance team of the correct treatment of this situation.

8 Inventory valuation

In this chapter you will learn how to:

- calculate inventory values using FIFO and AVCO methods

- explain why different methods of inventory valuation produce different profit figures in the short term

- assess the benefits and drawbacks of using FIFO and AVCO

- reconcile inventory values with actual inventory.

Background knowledge

Valuing inventory is important as it appears on both the income statement and on the statement of financial position (balance sheet). If the value placed on the closing inventory is too high then both the profit and the assets will be overstated and vice versa if the inventory is too low.

Key terms

JIT: just in time is an increasingly popular method of handling inventory where the minimum amount of inventory is held and replenished as required.

FIFO: the first in first out method involves the oldest costs being used first when inventory is issued.

Periodic method: this is when inventory is valued at the end of a financial period. It is the quickest method and should always be used when calculating the FIFO method even when perpetual is asked for as the same answer is found.

For many companies inventory can be a major part of the expenditure in the income statement and of the assets on the statement of financial position (balance sheet). Some companies do seek to minimise the amount of inventory that they hold by using methods such as just in time (**JIT**), which means holding the bare minimum amount of inventory and thus avoiding issues such as storage costs, security costs, theft and items perishing or going out of date. The valuation of inventory is covered in IAS 2 Inventories and means that inventory should be valued at the lower of cost (what we paid and other associated costs such as carriage inwards) or net realisable value (expected selling price less any expenses to achieve saleable condition). As with the previous chapter on accounting standards it is worth refreshing your understanding of accounting concepts in particular prudence, consistency and other payables (accruals) concept. It is important that these concepts are adhered to in order to produce the most accurate inventory valuation which is also acceptable by the Companies Act 1985 and IAS 2 Inventories.

Case study

Sharp Edges Ltd

Sharp Edges Ltd supplies chainsaws for tree surgeons. A new accountant has been appointed. The managing director would like the inventory of chainsaws to be valued at the price he intends to sell at. The accountant disagrees with this valuation but is concerned that the average cost method (AVCO) has been used, which he considers to be more time consuming than first in first out (FIFO).

FIFO

First in first out (**FIFO**) inventory valuation involves the assumption that the inventory bought first is used first. This is just in terms of the value of the inventory and does not mean that we must physically rotate our inventory (which a lot of companies do anyway). Any remaining inventory is valued much closer to the current cost using this method. FIFO produces the same result whether the **periodic** or **perpetual method** is used. The perpetual method involves keeping a running balance of inventory and its value, which is more time consuming than the periodic method that is shown next. Always use the periodic method with FIFO as the result is the same and it takes less time.

Illustration

First in first out method

The following information is available for Sharp Edges Ltd for the three months ended 30 June 2013.

On 1 April 2013 they had two chainsaws in inventory that had cost £200 each.

Date	Purchases	Sales
3 April	3 @ £210	
6 April		2 @ £300
22 May	4 @ £220	
26 May		2 @ £300
9 June		1 @ £300
13 June	2 @ £230	

Fig. 8.1 *Inventory movements*

It is important to remember to include any opening inventory when performing inventory valuations. Unless you are required to calculate profit you must ignore the selling price of the inventory as this is irrelevant unless the item can only be sold for less than it was bought for.

	Units
Opening inventory if any	2
Add number of purchases/receipts	9
Less number of sales/issues	5
Closing inventory	6

Fig. 8.2 *FIFO method*

The table measures the inventory in units. Because we are using the FIFO method we have sold our 'oldest' inventory first so are now left with (2 @ £230 + 4 @ £220) = £1,340. Do not make the mistake of costing all six units at £230 as you only bought two at that cost.

FIFO is the most widely used inventory valuation method as it is the easiest to calculate and understand, it is acceptable for tax purposes and IAS 2 Inventories, and the inventory remaining is valued at the most recent costs paid. This is useful for costing a job for a customer as it ensures the company are using relevant and up-to-date costs to quote to the customer. This enables the company to make profitable decisions in their planning. The issue costs of inventory are based on actual costs unlike AVCO, which as you will see can produce costs that were never actually paid.

AVCO

The average cost method, **AVCO**, is just what it says: each time a new batch of inventory is purchased we need to calculate a new value for it based on average costs.

Key terms

Perpetual method: a running balance is kept using this method and a new value of inventory is calculated each time inventory is received or issued.

AVCO: the weighted average cost method involves a new value of inventory being calculated each time a different cost is paid. This new cost is then used for issues until a new receipt of inventory is made.

Activities

1. Some companies such as Stoves Ltd, who make ovens, hold zero amounts of inventory as they have already sold the ovens that they are producing. What could be the advantages and disadvantages of this approach?

2. Explain to the managing director of Sharp Edges Ltd why the inventory cannot be valued at its selling price.

Illustration

Average cost method

	Received	Issued	Average cost per unit	Number of units	Inventory balance
3 January	10 @ £18		£18	10	£180
12 January	15 @ £18.50		£18.30	25	£457.50
18 January		8 @ £18.30	£18.30	17	£311.10
22 January	8 @ £19				
25 January		10 @			
30 January	9 @ £20				

Fig. 8.3 *AVCO method*

When we buy more inventory on 12 January we then need to recalculate. We do this by working out the total we have paid for inventory so far and then divide by the total number of units we now have.

$$\frac{(10 \times 18) + (15 \times £18.50)}{25} = £18.30$$

$10 \times 18 = 180$ is the amount of inventory we received on 3 January multiplied by the cost. This needs adding to the inventory on 12 January, which is $15 \times 18.50 = £277.50$ giving a total of £457.50. Then divide 457.50 by 25, which is the amount of inventory in units, giving the answer of £18.30.

Activity

3 Complete the AVCO table for January in Fig. 8.3.

Advantages and disadvantages of AVCO

Table 1 *AVCO*

Advantages	Disadvantages
Recognises that all issues from inventory are of equal value	New calculation required with each purchase of inventory
Averages out changes in prices	Prices charged with issues will not agree with prices actually paid
Acceptable for tax purposes and IAS 2 Inventories	The profit that results is lower than the FIFO method

Study tip

FIFO does not mean that we have to physically rotate the inventory, it is the oldest cost of inventory we use first rather than the actual inventory. A common error is that candidates confuse the physical movement of inventory with the inventory valuation for accounting purposes.

Activity

4 Advise the new accountant for Sharp Edges Ltd as to which method of inventory valuation he should use.

Effects on profit

In the long term, the profits will be the same over the life of the company, regardless of whether FIFO or AVCO are used, as all inventory will be used up at all the prices paid for it. The difference comes in the short term, where FIFO produces higher profits and AVCO lower. This may make you think, because of prudence, that it would be better to not overstate profits and use the AVCO method; both, though, are acceptable. What should not be done (in line with the concept of consistency) is to frequently change between the two as this then makes comparisons over years difficult. It is worth noting that the inventory valuation we use, whilst affecting our profit, does not affect our cash position. This is because we are still actually paying the same amount for the inventory, regardless of how we then go on to value it.

Illustration

Comparing FIFO and AVCO

The accountant for Sharp Edges Ltd has decided to compare the profit achieved for July using FIFO and AVCO to aid in his decision-making.

Date	Purchases	Sales
6 July	6 @ £230	
10 July	2 @ £240	
15 July		4 @ £350
24 July	5 @ £260	

Fig. 8.4 *Inventory movements for July*

There were no units remaining at the start of July.

	Units
Opening inventory if any	0
Add number of purchases/receipts	13
Less number of sales/issues	4
Closing inventory	9

Fig. 8.5 *Method for FIFO*

Sharp Edges Ltd had 0 units at the start of the month, they purchased 13 and sold 4 so are left with 9 units, 5 @ £260, 2 @ £240 and 2 @ £230, so the closing inventory valuation using FIFO is £2,240.

	Received	Issued	Average cost per unit	Number of units	Inventory balance
6 July	6 @ £230		£230	6	£1,380
10 July	2 @ £240		£232.50	8	£1,860
15 July		4 @ £232.50	£232.50	4	£930
24 July	5 @ £260		£247.78	9	£2,230

Fig. 8.6 *Method for AVCO*

The income statements (first section) can now be completed so that a comparison can be made.

	FIFO		AVCO	
	£	£	£	£
Revenue		1,400		1,400
Cost of sales				
Purchases	3,160		3,160	
Less: closing inventory	(2,240)	920	(2,230)	930
Gross profit		480		470

Fig. 8.7 *Income statements (first section) to compare FIFO and AVCO*

Revenue is calculated by multiplying the number of units sold, 4, by the selling price of £350.

Link

In AS Unit 2 you will have studied the key concepts needed for inventory valuation, which are prudence, consistency and other payables (accruals) concepts. You will have also learnt markup and margin, which is useful for converting selling price back to cost price.

Show the skills

The skill involved in inventory valuation is being able to sample enough of the inventory so that an accurate extrapolation can be made. If the sampling matches what the business states then you can be reasonably happy that the valuation is true and fair. This is why an auditor can never state that the financial statements are 100% accurate. It would be physically impossible for an audit team to count every item of the inventory for a large business. The concept of prudence is key for this area as overvaluing inventory affects both the income statement and the statement of financial position (balance sheet). New businesses often assume that the value of the inventory is what it could be sold for. The reality is that inventory can often lose value rapidly due to it being perishable, fashionable or technological.

Purchases are calculated by multiplying each order of inventory received by the cost so, $6 \times £230 = £1,380$, $2 \times £240 = £480$ and $5 \times £260 = £1,300$ totalled $= £3,160$.

Notice that the sales and purchases are the same regardless of the inventory valuation method used.

The income statements (first section) show that gross profit is higher by £10 (£480 – £470), if the FIFO method is used. Total profits over the life of the business will be the same whichever method is chosen since all inventory will be sold.

If you need to alter the gross profit to show the effect of a change in inventory calculation simply subtract the 'old' inventory amount from the gross profit and add the 'new' inventory. You should find FIFO is producing the highest profit.

Inventory valuation and the statement of financial position (balance sheet) date

In an ideal world all counting and valuing of inventory would take place on the last day of the accounting period. This is sometimes impossible so adjustments have to be made to discover the actual inventory held on the correct date. It could be that the inventory valuation is having to take place earlier than it should and in this case adjustments are needed but the opposite way to the approach shown here. Always think about where the inventory should have been on the day of the inventory valuation and where it actually was. If it should have been included it needs adding and if it would not have been in the warehouse or stockroom it needs subtracting.

Illustration

Approach to adjusting inventory

Lozzie plc has a financial year end on 31 December 2012. The inventory valuation is not performed until 8 January 2013. The valuation on that date is £32,050. The following information is available:

1 Selling price is cost price + 25%.

   We must not calculate the inventory at selling price so will need to divide by 1.25 whenever we are given selling price to find the cost. If the markup was 30% we would divide by 1.3 and so on.

2 Purchases since 31 December 2012 amounted to £4,500.

   Ask yourself: where was that inventory on 31 December? Not in Lozzie plc's stockroom!

3 Returns inwards or sales returns since 31 December 2012 were £400 at selling price.

   Did we know on 31 December that we would be receiving this inventory back? No, so it needs subtracting. Remember to convert £400 to cost. So, $\frac{400}{1.25} = 320$.

4 Free samples of £57 had been included.

   Inventory should be valued at the lower of cost or net realisable value. If an item was free that makes its cost 0 so it should not be included in the inventory valuation.

5 Rain had damaged inventory that originally cost £600 and is now worth £80.

Apply the same logic as you did in item 4. We need to subtract £520 to reflect the fall in value.

6 Goods with a selling price of £420 had been sent on a **sale or return** basis to one of Lozzie's customers on 20 December 2012.

Sale or return is particularly useful for smaller businesses who may not have enough finance to buy sufficient inventory. It means that the seller displays the inventory and if they sell it they will pay the supplier and if they don't sell after a certain time period they will return it to the supplier. Who does the inventory belong to on 31 December? Unless the customer has sold it, it still belongs to Lozzie plc. Again, convert selling price to cost.

7 Invoices totalling £2,420 were sent out for goods sold during the first week in January 2013.

Where was that inventory on 31 December? In Lozzie plc's stockroom, so it needs adding back after adjusting to the cost figure.

We can now enter the above information in the following statement.

Lozzie plc statement to show corrected inventory value at 31 December 2012

	£	£	£
Valuation 8 January 2013			32,050
	Increase	Decrease	
Purchases		4,500	
Sales returns		320	
Free samples		57	
Damaged inventory		520	
Sale or return	336		
Sales	1,936		
Net increase/decrease	2,272	5,397	(3,125)
Inventory valuation at 31 December 2013			28,925

Fig. 8.8 *Adjusting inventory*

Key term

Sale or return: goods are supplied and do not need to be paid for until they are sold and can be returned to the supplier if they don't sell. They still belong to the supplier and should be included in their inventory.

Study tip

The periodic method can always be used for FIFO as it produces the same inventory valuation as the perpetual method, so save some time.

In this chapter you will have learnt:

- how to calculate inventory values using FIFO and AVCO
- the benefits and drawbacks of each method and how they affect the profit
- how to make adjustments for early or late inventory valuation.

Practice questions

1   Salema Begum owns and runs an office supplies business. She has always used the weighted average cost (AVCO) method of inventory valuation. Her younger brother Rezah is studying accounting at college and is convinced that Salema could increase her profits by using the first in first out (FIFO) method.

(a)   Assess the effect each of the two methods of inventory valuation would have on profits:
   (i)   in the short term
   (ii) in the long term.

(b)   Explain whether or not Salema should change the method of inventory valuation she has been using in order to alter:
   (i)   profits
   (ii) cash flow.

2   Craig Taylor cannot decide whether to use FIFO or AVCO for the inventory valuation of the canisters in his scuba diving business and provides the following:

Date	Purchases	Sales
1 September	10 @ £15	
2 September		4 @ £40
14 September	8 @ £17	
16 September	4 @ £18	
19 September		17 @ £40
24 September	9 @ £19	

He had two canisters on 31 August which he had bought for £14.

(a)   Calculate the closing inventory balance using both the FIFO and AVCO approaches.

(b)   Prepare an income statement (trading section) for each method, using your results from (a).

3   Millbrook Ltd sells fir trees. At 1 December 2012, there were 120 trees in stock, which cost a total of £1,800.

During December 2012 the following transactions took place:

Date	Purchases	Sales
4 December	150 @ £24	
12 December		200 @ £35
16 December	220 @ £26.50	
18 December		270 @ £45

Millbrook Ltd uses the AVCO method of valuing inventory. Using this method, inventory at 31 December 2012 was valued at £500. The directors are considering changing the method of inventory valuation to the FIFO method.

(a) Calculate the value of inventory at 31 December 2012 using the FIFO method.

(b) Calculate the gross profit for the month ending 31 December 2012 using both the FIFO and AVCO methods. (Note: use the opening inventory valuation of £1,800 for both calculations.)

4 Amy sells patio heaters. During September 2012, the following transactions took place.

Date	Purchases	Sales
3 September	10 units @ £270 each	
11 September		16 units
22 September	8 units @ £257.50 each	
29 September		18 units

At 1 September 2012, there were 20 units in stock, which cost £4,200 in total.

Amy calculates her selling price to achieve a 75% gross profit margin.

(a) Calculate the value of inventory at 30 September 2012 using the AVCO method.

(b) Prepare an extract from the income statement for the month ended 30 September, to show the gross profit.

5 Always Friday plc has an accounting year ended 30 November 2013. At the end of November the store manager was ill and was unable to count the inventory until the close of business on 12 December 2013. At that date the inventory was valued at £105,980. The selling price of all goods is based on a 20% markup on cost.

The following information relates to 1–12 December 2013.

▪ Included in the inventory valuation were goods at a cost of £1,200 that had been damaged and were now worth £500.

▪ Sales invoices for goods sent in that period totalled £24,000.

▪ The company was sent a batch of free samples. They had been included at the price of £352.

▪ Purchases of inventory were £12,500.

▪ Sales returned by customers were £5,100 at selling price.

▪ The marketing department have currently borrowed inventory worth £600 for a trade fair. This inventory has been included in the inventory at 12 December 2013.

(a) Calculate the value of closing inventory to be included in Always Friday plc's financial statements at 30 November 2013.

(b) Explain two reasons why a physical inventory valuation will often provide a different figure compared with an inventory figure as per the computer inventory system.

6 AQA ACC3 January 2013

Contador Ltd had its financial year end on 31 October 2012. It was impossible to carry out a stocktake on this date. However, a stocktake was carried out after the year end on 12 November 2012 when inventory was valued at £31,300.

The following transactions took place between 1 and 12 November 2012.

Date	Transaction
2 November	Goods with a cost price of £31,000 were returned to a supplier.
4 November	Goods with a cost price of £39,500 were purchased from a supplier.
7 November	Goods with a selling price of £121,440 were sold to a customer.
11 November	Goods with a selling price of £118,600 were returned by a customer.

No other transactions took place during the period.

Selling prices for goods are based on cost price plus a uniform markup of 20%.

(a)   Calculate the value of closing inventory at 31 October 2012.

Inventory is currently valued using the FIFO method. Using this method, the gross profit for the business was calculated as £9,240 for the period from 1 to 12 November 2012. The closing inventory using the AVCO method would be £31,100 at 12 November 2012. The directors of Contador Ltd are unsure about whether to change from the FIFO method to the AVCO method.

(b)   Calculate the gross profit for the period from 1 to 12 November 2012 using the AVCO method.

(c)   Explain two reasons why the directors should not change from the FIFO method to the AVCO method.

Further aspects of management accounting

Introduction to Unit 4

Unit 4 will develop your understanding and skills in relation to management accounting. For the first time you will look at organisations that manufacture products. Once you are familiar with the financial statements for manufacturing organisations, you will be able to move on to study a variety of costing concepts and techniques. For example, you will study marginal costing, which enables appropriate decisions to be made when a variety of courses of action are available to a manufacturing organisation. This unit also introduces two techniques that are used by businesses when deciding how best to invest substantial amounts of finance in developing new products, replacing plant and equipment, etc. You will return to the subject of budgeting that was introduced in Unit 2 when you learned about cash budgets, but you will look at other types of budget – for example, production budgets and labour budgets. Finally, you will investigate the wider context for business decision-making, and learn about some of the other, non-financial factors, including ethical factors, that might influence business decisions.

Chapter 9 – Manufacturing accounts

This chapter will introduce manufacturing organisations. You will learn how to prepare end-of-year financial statements for manufacturers with sophisticated techniques to show not only gross profit and profit for the year, but the profit made from manufacturing as well.

Chapter 10 – Marginal costing

You will gain an understanding of how costs can be categorised and of important concepts including contribution, break-even and marginal cost. You will study techniques that enable businesses to make choices between alternative courses of action. For example, you will be able to decide which products a manufacturer should make when faced with a scarcity of certain resources, such as materials or skilled labour.

Chapter 11 – Absorption costing

This chapter looks at absorption costing, which is an alternative way of viewing manufacturing costs. You will learn how it is possible to make sure that all a business's costs are passed on to customers when pricing particular products or projects.

Chapter 12 – Activity-based costing

This chapter will introduce activity-based costing (ABC). This process produces more accurate cost information and enables management to have a greater understanding of why costs are incurred.

Chapter 13 – Standard costing and variance analysis

This chapter introduces the concept of standard costing. You will develop skills in using a technique, called variance analysis, which makes it possible for the management of a manufacturing organisation to identify unexpected changes in the cost of materials and labour. You will learn how to explain why such variations in cost might occur and how to calculate the effect of the changes on the budgeted profit of the organisation.

Chapter 14 – Capital investment appraisal

You will study two techniques that help guide managers when choosing between alternative capital investment projects. You will learn how to calculate net cash flows for projects. You will then develop skills in assessing the impact of different projects, taking account of how quickly the money invested is paid back, and the real value of the cash flows taking account of the time value of money – the idea that money received some time in the future is not as valuable to an organisation as money received now. You will learn about the respective advantages and disadvantages of each technique and how to make recommendations as to which project should be chosen taking account of appropriate financial analysis.

Chapter 15 – Budgeting

This chapter builds on the knowledge of budgeting you gained in Unit 2. You will learn how to prepare a wide variety of budgets including those for trade receivables, trade payables, production, sales, etc., and how they contribute to a business's master budget.

Chapter 16 – Social accounting

You will look at business decisions from a wider point of view than just financial gain, taking account of how these decisions might affect various stakeholders including employees, and also the national economy, the environment, etc.

When you are assessed on this unit, you will be expected to demonstrate an understanding of the wide variety of techniques that have been covered, applying these to a variety of business problems. As always, well-organised and presented answers will be expected. As you would expect in a unit that is concerned with decision-making, you will also be expected to write explanations and reports in which you assess various courses of action. You will be assessed on how effectively you weigh up the benefits and potential disadvantages of the available options, and make recommendations drawing on the results of the analysis you have undertaken. As you know, at A2 level a generally higher standard is expected in all the skills on which you are assessed.

9 Manufacturing accounts

So far during your AS and A2 studies you have developed skills in preparing the accounts of several business structures: sole traders, partnerships and limited companies. These businesses have shared a common trait, namely they have all been retailers. However, not all businesses are retailers, whereby a completed good is purchased from a supplier and then sold on to a customer. Many businesses actually manufacture their own products which, when finished, are then sold on to customers. The financial statements for a manufacturing business differ from those of a retailer, as the costs associated with the manufacturing process have to be identified and recorded separately to the non-manufacturing costs. This chapter will introduce you to manufacturing companies and their accounts.

Topic 1 — Introduction to the financial statements of a manufacturer

In this topic you will learn how to:

- prepare a manufacturing account showing the prime cost, work in progress and production cost of manufactured goods
- distinguish between direct and indirect costs
- prepare the financial statements for a manufacturing organisation.

Key terms

Manufacturing account: an account prepared to calculate the production cost of manufactured goods.

Prime costs: the total of all direct costs incurred when producing the products.

Direct costs: this cost is identified with the cost unit. Costs attributable to a particular product, e.g. direct materials and direct labour.

Case study

Matthias Manufacturing Ltd
Matthias Manufacturing Ltd produces wooden garden furniture. All products are manufactured within one factory and then sold to a variety of retailers from garden nurseries to well-known chain stores.

The manufacturing account

What is a manufacturing account?

A retailer buys and sells completed products, whereas a manufacturer has to produce the products to sell. A **manufacturing account** is therefore prepared to show all the costs associated with the making of these products within the factory.

A simple manufacturing account is split into two sections:

- the **prime cost** section, which calculates the total of the direct manufacturing cost of the products, and the **direct costs**, which include raw materials, direct labour and royalties
- the **manufacturing overheads** section, which identifies all the other costs associated with the production of the products, for example factory rent, machine maintenance and machine depreciation.

When these sections are combined the **production cost of manufactured goods** can be found.

Activity

1 Identify three manufacturing businesses. For each business give three examples of an indirect cost.

Study tip

Ensure that the manufacturing account only includes information about the factory and actual manufacturing process and not other non-production costs such as warehouse, administration, finance or distribution costs.

Illustration

How to prepare a simple manufacturing account from a trial balance

On 31 December 2013 an extract of the trial balance of Matthias Manufacturing Ltd was as follows.

Trial balance extract for Matthias Manufacturing Ltd at 31 December 2013

	£	£
Carriage inwards	2,200	
Carriage outwards	1,800	
Depreciation of manufacturing machinery	11,100	
Factory rent	20,100	
Inventory of raw materials at 1 January 2013	17,400	
Inventory of raw materials at 31 December 2013	19,500	
Manufacturing royalties	14,500	
Manufacturing wages	54,600	
Other factory overheads	32,000	
Purchases of raw materials	62,300	
Returns inwards	5,300	
Returns outwards		6,700
Revenue		334,000

Fig. 9.1 *Trial balance extract*

The manufacturing account for Matthias Manufacturing Ltd for the year ended 31 December 2013 was drawn up.

Manufacturing account for Matthias Manufacturing Ltd for year ended 31 December 2013

	£	£
Inventory of raw materials at 1 January 2013		17,400
Purchases of raw materials	62,300	
Carriage inwards	2,200	
Returns outwards	(6,700)	
Net purchases of raw materials		57,800
		75,200
Inventory of raw materials at 31 December 2013		(19,500)
Cost of raw materials consumed		55,700
Manufacturing wages		54,600
Manufacturing royalties		14,500
Prime cost		124,800

(Continued)

Depreciation of manufacturing machinery		11,100
Factory rent		20,100
Other factory overheads		32,000
		188,000

Fig. 9.2 *Manufacturing account*

What is work in progress?

Manufacturing is a continuous process and so not all goods are complete at the end of financial period. The partly finished goods are referred to as inventory of **work in progress**.

The total production cost of manufactured goods in a manufacturing account is therefore made up of:

prime cost + factory overheads + opening work in progress – closing work in progress

Illustration

How to prepare a manufacturing account including inventory of work in progress

The inventory of work in progress for Matthias Manufacturing Ltd for the year ended 31 December 2013 was:

- inventory of work in progress at 1 January 2013: £12,500
- inventory of work in progress at 31 December 2013: £14,200.

Manufacturing account continued for Matthias Manufacturing Ltd for year ended 31 December 2013

	£
b/fwd	188,000
Inventory of work in progress at 1 January 2013	12,500
Inventory of work in progress at 31 December 2013	(14,200)
Production cost of manufactured goods	186,300

Fig. 9.3 *Manufacturing account continued*

Income statement

Preparing a manufacturer's income statement (first section)

At the end of the production process the total production cost of manufactured goods is transferred to the income statement (first section). This figure replaces the purchases of goods for resale within the calculation of cost of sales (cost of goods sold).

The completed goods are referred to as **finished goods**. These are placed in the income statement (first section) within the calculation of cost of sales (cost of goods sold).

Inventory of work in progress: It should be noted that in the manufacturing account the inventory of work in progress is treated as any other type of inventory, namely opening inventory is added to and closing inventory is subtracted from the calculation for production cost of manufactured goods.

Show the skills

When asked to prepare a manufacturing account remember that it is a sequential record of the production process, starting from raw materials through production costs to work in progress and the total production cost of manufactured goods. The layout must be learned.

Explanatory note

The income statement (first section) of a manufacturer is similar to that of a non-manufacturing organisation. The inventory recorded is the finished goods, but the main difference is that purchases of goods for resale is replaced by the production cost of manufactured goods from the manufacturing account.

Link

For more information on either the valuation of inventory or the prudence and realisation concepts, see *AQA Accounting AS*, Chapter 6.

Illustration

How to prepare an income statement for a manufacturing business

The inventory of finished goods for Matthias Manufacturing Ltd for the year ended 31 December 2013 was:

- inventory of finished goods at 1 January 2013: £25,100
- inventory of finished goods at 31 December 2013: £29,400.

Income statement (first section) for Matthias Manufacturing Ltd for the year ended 31 December 2013

	£	£
Revenue		334,000
Returns inwards		(5,300)
Net revenue		328,700
Opening inventory of finished goods	25,100	
Production cost of manufactured goods	186,300	
	211,400	
Closing inventory of finished goods	(29,400)	
Cost of sales (cost of goods sold)		(182,000)
Gross profit		146,700

Fig. 9.4 *Income statement (first section)*

Statement of financial position (balance sheet)

How is inventory recorded in the statement of financial position (balance sheet) of a manufacturer compared to that of a retailer?

There are *three* types of inventory within a manufacturing business:

- inventory of raw materials
- inventory of work in progress
- inventory of finished goods.

The statement of financial position (balance sheet) for a manufacturing business therefore has to show all three types of inventory held at the year end within the current assets, whereas a retailer has only *one* type of inventory, namely finished goods.

Statement of financial position (balance sheet) extract for Matthias Manufacturing Ltd at 31 December 2013

	£
Current assets:	
Inventory of raw materials	19,500
Inventory of work in progress	14,200
Inventory of finished goods	29,400
	63,100

Fig. 9.5 *Statement of financial position (balance sheet) extract*

All of the inventory in the current assets is valued at the lower of cost and net realisable value. This continues the application of the prudence and realisation concepts. This will further be illustrated in the next topic on unrealised profit.

In this topic you will have learnt:

- how to prepare a manufacturing account to show the important subtotals, including prime cost and total overheads
- how to distinguish between direct costs and indirect costs
- how to prepare a manufacturing account to include work in progress
- how to prepare a full set of financial statements for a manufacturing organisation.

Practice questions

1   Identify which of the following costs are either direct or indirect manufacturing costs.

Cost	Direct	Indirect
Cost of raw materials		
Factory supervisor salary		
Lease of factory		
Machine depreciation		
Royalties		

2   The following information is available for Brown Ltd, a manufacturer of toy wooden soldiers, for the year ended 31 March 2013.

	£
Direct wages	133,600
Factory insurance	14,800
Inventory of raw materials at 1 April 2012	42,500
Inventory of raw materials at 31 March 2013	51,200
Factory rent	39,000
Purchases of raw materials	98,100
Royalties	15,000

Additional information:

- At 31 March 2013 direct wages due were £16,400.
- Factory rent was payable a month in advance. The monthly rent was £3,000.
- An invoice for purchases of raw materials of £1,200 had been omitted.
- The inventory of raw materials at 31 March 2013 included inventory which had cost £5,500. This had been damaged in transit to the factory and was only now £3,600.

Prepare an extract from the manufacturing account to show the prime cost for the year ended 31 March 2013.

3   AQA ACC3 June 2003 (adapted)

Carroll Ltd is a manufacturing business making sunglasses. The following figures have been extracted from the company's ledgers at the year end 31 May 2013.

	£
Administration costs	36,750
Carriage inwards	16,550
Direct labour	264,100
Distribution costs	28,300
Factory overheads	114,050
Inventory at 1 June 2012:	
– raw materials	11,450
– work in progress	14,700
– finished goods	38,600
Purchases of raw materials	189,300
Returns inwards	1,600
Returns outwards	3,150

Additional information

At 31 May 2013 inventory was valued as follows:

	£
Raw material	14,150
Work in progress	18,300
Finished goods	45,700

▨ At 31 May 2013 direct wages accrued and unpaid amounted to £2,500.

▨ The factory overheads included an invoice for rent for the property (premises). This amounted to £48,000. However, only 75% was for the rent of the factory and the rest was for the rent of the offices and despatch warehouses.

▨ Carroll Ltd manufactures 300,000 pairs of sunglasses a year. The selling price of each pair is based on manufacturing cost plus 300%.

(a)   Explain what is meant by 'work in progress'.

(b)   Prepare the manufacturing account for Carroll Ltd for the year ended 31 May 2013.

(c)   Calculate the selling price per pair of sunglasses.

4   Studds plc manufactures rugby boots. The following information is available for Studds plc for the year ended 31 January 2013.

	£000
Carriage inwards	15
Carriage outwards	21
Factory wages	360
Heating and lighting	68
Inventory at 1 February 2012:	
– raw materials	42
– work in progress	18
– finished goods	84
Machinery at cost	340
Office equipment at cost	90
Office salaries	145
Power	110
Purchases of raw materials	567
Rent and rates	84
Royalties	16
Revenue	1,246

Additional information:

The inventory at 31 January 2013 were as follows.

	£000
Raw material	65
Work in progress	22
Finished goods	98

- 60% of the factory wages are direct and the rest are indirect
- 75% of both the heating and lighting and rent and rates are to be allocated to the factory and the rest to the office
- 80% of the power costs are to be allocated to the factory
- depreciation is to be charged on the machinery at 20% per annum using the straight-line method
- depreciation is to be charged on the office equipment at 10% per annum using the straight-line method.
- The valuation of finished goods at 31 January 2013 included goods that had been sold but not yet despatched, worth £12,000. The sales invoice had been recorded within the ledgers.

(a)   Prepare a manufacturing account for the year ended 31 January 2013.

(b)   Prepare an income statement for the year ended 31 January 2013.

(c)   Prepare an extract from the statement of financial position (balance sheet) as at 31 January 2013 to show the inventories held at the year end.

Topic 2   Manufacturing profit

In this topic you will learn how to:

- explain why some manufacturers include a manufacturing profit

- prepare the financial statements of a manufacturer to include manufacturing profit

- explain why it is necessary to make a provision for unrealised profit

- calculate the provision for unrealised profit

- prepare the financial statements of a manufacturer to include entries for both the manufacturing profit and the change in the provision for unrealised profit

- prepare the statement of financial position (balance sheet) recording inventory adjusted for the provision for unrealised profit.

Key terms

Transfer price: production cost of completed goods plus a percentage markup.

Factory profit, or manufacturing profit: the difference between the transfer price and the production cost of completed goods, or the amount of markup.

Link

For more information on markup, see *AQA Accounting AS*, Chapter 9.

Case study

Danil Doors Manufacturing Ltd

Danil Doors Manufacturing Ltd produces wooden doors. All doors are sold to the national market.

The recording of manufacturing profit

What is manufacturing profit?

Some manufacturing businesses transfer their products from the factory to the income statement (first section) at total production cost plus a notional markup percentage. This is referred to as the **transfer price**. The difference between the production cost of completed goods and the transfer price is called **factory profit, or manufacturing profit**.

What are the benefits of using a transfer price?

- This process does not increase the overall profits of the business and merely identifies the profit made by particular cost centres.

- In this way the profit from the manufacturing is separated from the trading profit made elsewhere within the business. The part that the factory contributes to the overall profitability of the business is recognised.

- This allows the unit cost of goods manufactured to be compared with the cost of buying in completed goods from an outside source and enables a manager to evaluate a 'make or buy' decision.

What are the drawbacks of using a transfer price?

- The profit loaded transfer price should be realistic so direct comparisons with the cost of buying in goods can be made. However, there is a risk of an unrealistic view of the factory profitability being given unless other production prices are researched and used to set the transfer price.

- This technique does not improve overall the profitability of the business, rather it just splits the total profit between different cost centres.

- If a set percentage is used to calculate the transfer price this may fail to motivate factory managers and other workers, especially if their bonuses are dependent on the amount of factory profit.

Recording manufacturing profit

A manufacturing profit is recorded at the end of the manufacturing account. The transfer price then replaces purchases of goods for resale within the income statement (first section).

Illustration

How to prepare a manufacturing account with a manufacturing profit and a transfer price

Danil Doors Manufacturing Ltd transfers doors from the factory to the income statement (first section) at cost plus 20%.

On 31 March 2013 the company's trial balance was as follows.

Information for Danil Doors Manufacturing Ltd for year ended 31 March 2013

	£
Factory overheads	257,600
Factory wages	390,000
Inventory of finished goods at 1 April 2012 (at cost plus 20%)	108,000
Inventory of finished goods at 31 March 2013 (at cost plus 20%)	126,000
Inventory of raw materials at 1 April 2012	63,400
Inventory of raw materials at 31 March 2013	71,200
Inventory of work in progress at 1 April 2012	16,400
Inventory of work in progress at 31 March 2013	18,100
Provision for unrealised profit at 1 April 2012	1,800
Purchases of raw materials	220,900
Revenue	1,210,000

Fig. 9.6 *Trial balance*

Additional information:

■ Factory wages owed amounted to £10,000.
■ The factory wages are apportioned $\frac{3}{4}$ to direct labour and the rest is indirect.

The manufacturing account for Danil Doors Manufacturing Ltd for the year ended 31 March 2013 was drawn up.

Manufacturing account for Danil Doors Manufacturing Ltd for the year ended 31 March 2013

	£
Inventory of raw materials at 1 April 2012	63,400
Purchases of raw materials	220,900
Inventory of raw materials at 31 March 2013	(71,200)
Cost of materials consumed	213,100
Direct wages	300,000
Prime cost	513,100
Indirect wages	100,000
Factory overheads	257,600
	870,700
Inventory of work in progress at 1 April 2012	16,400
Inventory of work in progress at 31 March 2013	(18,100)
Production cost of manufactured goods	869,000
Factory profit at 20%	173,800
Transfer price	1,042,800

Fig. 9.7 *Manufacturing account*

The provision for unrealised profit

Why is it necessary to create a provision for unrealised profit?

As you have previously studied, IAS 2 requires that inventory is valued at the lower of cost and net realisable value. In the statement of financial position (balance sheet) inventories of finished goods should be shown at the cost of production and therefore if a transfer price is used these inventories will include an element of **unrealised profit on finished goods**. Unrealised profits should not be recognised within the statement of financial position (balance sheet) and financial statements as it contravenes both the realisation and prudence concepts.

A provision for unrealised profit is therefore used to:

- remove the unrealised profit in the income statement otherwise profits are overstated by the amount of unrealised profit
- remove the unrealised profit from the inventory of finished goods within the current assets on the statement of financial position (balance sheet) so that inventory is not overvalued and is valued at cost and not cost plus a percentage markup.

How is a provision for unrealised profit calculated?

When inventory of finished goods is valued at cost plus a percentage markup, the method for calculating the unrealised profit is

$$\frac{\text{inventory at cost plus profit percentage}}{100 + \text{profit percentage}} \times \text{percentage}$$

Illustration

How to calculate unrealised profit

At 31 March 2013 the inventory of finished goods was valued at £126,000, being cost plus the markup of 20%.

The amount of unrealised profit is therefore

$$\frac{£126,000}{(100 + 20)} \times 20 = £21,000$$

This approach can also be used to calculate the original cost of the inventory.

In the previous illustration the original cost of the inventory is

$$\frac{£126,000}{120} \times 100 = £105,000$$

These answers can be checked.

cost of inventory + unrealised profit = inventory of finished goods at cost plus markup percentage

$$£105,000 + £21,000 = £126,000$$

Activity

2 Calculate the amount of unrealised profit that is included in the following inventory values.

Table 1 *Inventory values*

Inventory values	Markup percentage
£	%
42,000	20
195,000	30

How is the provision for unrealised profit recorded in the statement of financial position (balance sheet)?

The inventory of finished goods is recorded at the cost price without the unrealised profit.

Illustration

How to record provision for unrealised profit in the statement of financial position (balance sheet)

An extract to show the inventory of finished goods in the statement of financial position (balance sheet) would be as follows.

Statement of financial position (balance sheet) extract for Danil Doors Manufacturing Ltd at 31 March 2013

	£	£
Current assets:		
Inventory of raw materials		71,200
Inventory of work in progress		18,100
Inventory of finished goods	126,000	
Less provision for unrealised profit	(21,000)	
		105,000
		194,300

Fig. 9.8 *Statement of financial position (balance sheet) extract*

Explanatory note

Whenever completing the current assets the original cost of inventory of finished goods should always be clearly identified. In this illustration it is £105,000. This complies with IAS 2 and the prudence and realisation concepts.

How is the provision for unrealised profit recorded in the income statement?

The provision for unrealised profit is recorded in the income statement (second section) as follows.

Table 2 *Provision for unrealised profit*

First year	Full amount subtracted from factory profit
Subsequent years	Increase in provision subtracted from factory profit
	Decrease in provision added to factory profit

Illustration

How to record provision for unrealised profit in the income statement

At 31 March 2012 the closing inventory for Danil Doors Manufacturing Ltd had been valued at £108,000, which included unrealised profit of £18,000.

The change in provision is recorded as follows.

	£
This year's provision for unrealised profit	21,000
Last year's provision for unrealised profit	18,000
Increase in provision	3,000

Fig. 9.9 *Change in provision*

This would be recorded in the income statement (first section) as follows.

Income statement (first section) for Danil Doors Manufacturing Ltd for the year ended 31 March 2013

	£	£
Revenue		1,210,000
Opening inventory of finished goods	108,000	
Transfer price	1,042,800	
Closing inventory of finished goods	(126,000)	
Cost of sales (cost of goods sold)		(1,024,800)
Gross profit		185,200
Factory profit	173,800	
Less increase in provision for unrealised profit	(3,000)	
		170,800

Fig. 9.10 *Income statement (first section)*

Explanatory notes

- Factory profit: This must be clearly identified within the financial statements as otherwise the profit is understated due to the inclusion of the transfer price instead of the production cost of manufactured goods.

- Increase in provision in unrealised profit: The increase in the provision in unrealised profit must also be clearly identified otherwise the factory profit is overstated. If there is a decrease in the provision then it should be added otherwise the factory profit is understated.

- If both the factory profit and provision for unrealised profit are included in the income statement then profit for the year will be the same as it would be if the business did not use a markup nor a transfer price.

Study tip

A common error in the examination is either to forget to bring forward the factory profit or to show the change in provision in isolation. These two adjustments should be recorded together.

In this topic you have learnt:

- why some manufacturers calculate a manufacturing profit
- to prepare a manufacturing account to include manufacturing profit
- why it is necessary to make a provision for unrealised profit
- how to calculate a provision for unrealised profit
- how to record a change in the provision for unrealised profit in the financial statement of a manufacturer
- how to record inventory adjusted for unrealised profit in the statement of financial position (balance sheet).

Practice questions

1 State the concepts identified with the provision for unrealised profit.

Concept 1..............................

Concept 2..............................

2 Complete the following table.

Inventory at cost	Markup	Inventory at transfer price
£	%	£
12,000	20	?
?	25	50,000

3 Louis Ltd manufactures a single product. His goods are transferred from the factory at cost plus 25%.

The following information is available at 31 October 2013.

	£
Inventory of finished goods at cost plus 25%	42,000
Inventory of raw materials	16,100
Inventory of work in progress	23,800

Prepare a statement of financial position (balance sheet) extract to show the inventory held by Louis Ltd at 31 October 2013.

4   AQA ACC3 January 2003 (adapted)

Pam's Products is a manufacturing business. It transfers all goods manufactured to the income statement at production cost plus 20%.

The following figures relate to inventory held by the business.

	As at 1 December 2012	As at 30 November 2013
	£	£
Inventories of:		
Raw materials	27,000	28,000
Work in progress	9,000	8,500
Finished goods	22,200	23,400
Provision for unrealised profit		

Required

(a)   Calculate the amount of provision for unrealised profit to be entered in the income statement for the year ended 30 November 2013.

What effect will the change have on the gross profit?

(b)   Show in detail how the information relating to all inventory should be shown on the statement of financial position (balance sheet) as at 30 November 2013.

Statement of financial position (balance sheet) extract for Pam's Products as at 30 November 2013	
	£
Current assets:	

(c)   Explain why it is necessary for Pam's Products to provide for unrealised profit.

5   AQA ACC3 January 2008 (adapted)

Donna owns and runs a manufacturing business. Goods are transferred from the manufacturing account to the income statement at cost plus 30%.

Donna provides the following information for the year ended 31 December 2013.

	£
Inventory of raw materials at:	
1 January 2013 (at cost)	14,700
31 December 2013 (at cost)	15,900
Inventory of finished goods at:	
1 January 2013 (at cost plus 30%)	22,100
31 December 2013 (at cost plus 30%)	24,700
Carriage inwards	1,450
Carriage outwards	2,375
Factory rent, rates and insurances	16,200
Factory wages	361,665
General factory overheads	33,045
Manufacturing machinery at cost	300,000
Manufacturing royalties	22,000
Provision for depreciation of manufacturing machinery at 1 January 2013	180,000
Provision for unrealised profit at 1 January 2013	5,100
Purchases of raw materials	317,600
Revenue	1,200,000

Additional information at 31 December 2013:

■   Manufacturing royalties paid in advance amounted to £500.

■   Factory wages are apportioned $\frac{2}{3}$ to direct labour and $\frac{1}{3}$ to indirect labour.

■   Factory insurances paid in advance amounted to £900.

■   Factory rates owed amounted to £850.

■   Depreciation on manufacturing machinery is to be charged at 10% per annum on a straight-line basis.

■   Work in progress has decreased by £900 over the year.

Required

(a)   Prepare a manufacturing account for the year ended 31 December 2013.

(b)   Calculate the amount to be entered in the income statement for the factory profit and the provision for unrealised profit for the year ended 31 December 2013.

Donna has said that gross profit has improved since she started to transfer goods from her manufacturing account to the income statement (first section) at cost plus 30%. 'I am now earning two lots of gross profit', she states.

However, Bob, one of her managers, says that he cannot see the point of marking up the goods to be transferred and he suggests that she discontinue the practice.

(c)   Advise Donna on whether or not she should continue to transfer goods from her factory at cost plus 30%.

6   Samuel Sandpiper manufactures car parts. Goods are transferred from the manufacturing account to the income statement at cost plus 20%. The following information is available for the year ended 31 March 2013.

Trial balance at 31 March 2013

	£	£
Administration and distribution costs	272,400	
Capital		120,000
Carriage inwards	1,800	
Cash and cash equivalents (bank and cash)		12,000
Factory overheads excluding rent	112,700	
Factory rent	48,000	
Factory wages	86,800	
Inventory at 1 April 2012:		
– raw materials	12,100	
– work in progress	24,600	
– finished goods	36,000	
Bank loan		10,000
Manufacturing machinery	242,000	
Manufacturing royalties	16,000	
Provision for depreciation on machinery at 1 April 2012		181,500
Provision for unrealised profit		6,000
Purchases of raw materials	69,900	
Returns inwards	5,200	
Revenue		610,800
Trade payables		43,700
Trade receivables	56,500	
	984,000	984,000

Additional information:

▪ Inventory at 31 March 2013:
   – raw materials   £10,600
   – work in progress   £26,200
   – finished goods   £35,400

▪ Factory rent prepaid for the year ending 31 March 2014 amounted to £3,000. The rent is to be apportioned $\frac{3}{5}$ to the manufacturing account and $\frac{2}{5}$ to the income statement.

▪ Depreciation on manufacturing machinery is to be charged at 15% per year on a straight-line basis.

▪ The bank loan is repayable on 1 September 2013.

▪ Outstanding factory wages at 31 March 2013 amounted to £2,400.

(a)   Prepare the manufacturing account for the year ended 31 March 2013.

(b)   Prepare the income statement for the year ended 31 March 2013.

(c)   Prepare the statement of financial position (balance sheet) at 31 March 2013.

10 Marginal costing

In this chapter you will learn how to:

- explain the terms 'marginal cost', 'direct cost', 'indirect cost', 'variable cost', 'semi-variable cost', 'fixed cost', 'contribution', 'break-even' and 'margin of safety'

- calculate a break-even point using the appropriate formula, and represent it on a graph

- explain the limitations of break-even analysis

- identify the uses and limitations of marginal costing

- select and apply relevant techniques using marginal costing to aid decision making.

Key terms

Marginal cost: the cost of one extra unit.

Variable cost: these costs vary with the level of production.

Fixed cost: these costs do not vary with the level of production.

Semi-variable costs: these costs are partly fixed and partly variable.

In Chapter 9 you gained an understanding of how to record the costs associated with a manufacturing process. But how are these costs calculated? Do costs all behave the same way? What information can costs give us? These questions lead us into the realm of management and cost accounting rather than financial accounting. Financial accounting deals purely with the recording of historical data whereas management and cost accounting deals with the information that will form the basis of decision-making and cost control for both the present day and the future. This chapter will introduce you to one of the methods used within cost accounting, namely marginal costing.

Case study

Stanley Harold Ltd
Stanley Harold Ltd manufactures golf balls and sells to an international market. The golf balls are sold in box sets of six.

Marginal costing

Marginal costing is a costing method that only considers **marginal costs**, which are those costs that are incurred when one extra unit is produced, for example the direct costs. Direct costs are those costs that can be identified with the actual production unit: namely the cost of direct material, cost of direct labour and any other **variable cost** that increases as production increases. Indirect costs are those costs that cannot be identified with the actual production unit and are not considered, for example staff administration costs.

The marginal costing method is used when:

- calculating the break-even point for a product
- considering whether to make or buy a product
- calculating the cost of a special order
- a business has a limiting factor that restricts its activities.

Types of costs

Within the marginal costing model it is important to distinguish between the different types of costs, as **fixed costs** are not considered.

- Variable costs: These costs vary in direct proportion with the level of production, for example direct wages and materials.
- Fixed costs: These costs do not vary in direct proportion to the level of production, for example rent payable, supervisors' salaries and insurance.
- **Semi-variable costs**: These costs are partly fixed and partly variable, for example telephone costs that have a fixed line rental but a variable call charge cost.

Study tip

Do not forget that marginal revenues could also be considered, which are those revenues received when one extra unit is sold.

Study tip

If you are asked to define a term try to use the exact definitions of the different types of cost and support these definitions with an example.

■ Activity

1 List five examples of each type of cost: variable, fixed and semi-variable.

■ Explanatory notes

- Layout: The layout clearly distinguishes between variable and fixed costs. The variable costs are made up of materials and labour.

- Material costs: In order to make the calculations easier the material costs at full price are shown separately to those with a discount. This method is recommended for examination questions.

- Labour costs: Once again in order to make calculations easier the labour costs are split between those with overtime and those without and at normal rates.

■ Illustration

How to apply the correct cost behaviour

Stanley Harold Ltd has provided the following information for the year ended 31 January 2013.

- During the year 60,000 sets of golf balls were produced.

- Each set of golf balls uses £4 worth of materials. The material suppliers allowed a cash discount if Stanley Harold Ltd paid early. Only 25% of materials were paid for taking advantage of this discount. Discounted materials cost £50,000. Material is a variable cost.

- Labour is paid for at a rate of £8 per hour. Unfortunately during the year orders could not be completed in normal working hours due to staff sickness. The directors of Stanley Harold Ltd agreed to pay overtime to workers so orders could be completed. The overtime was paid on 5,000 sets of golf balls at a rate of £16 per hour. Each set of golf balls takes 15 minutes to make. Labour is a variable cost.

- All other manufacturing costs were fixed and amounted to £300,000 for the year.

The manufacturing cost for the 60,000 sets of golf balls is therefore as follows.

	£
Material costs:	
With discount:	50,000
Without discount: 75% × 60,000 × £4	180,000
Labour costs:	
Overtime: 5,000 × (£16 × 0.25)	20,000
Without overtime: 55,000 × (£8 × 0.25)	110,000
Total variable costs	360,000
Fixed manufacturing costs	300,000
Total costs	660,000

Fig. 10.1 *Manufacturing cost*

From this illustration it is possible to further calculate useful costs. For example the total manufacturing cost per golf ball set is

$$\frac{£660,000}{60,000} = £11$$

Whereas the variable cost per golf ball can be calculated as

$$\frac{£360,000}{60,000} = £6$$

The fixed cost per golf ball set can therefore be calculated as

$$\frac{£300,000}{60,000} = £5$$

Contribution

The calculation of contribution is an important part of marginal costing as it identifies the amount of money made per unit towards covering fixed costs and profit. Once the fixed costs are covered, profit is made. **Contribution** is calculated as the difference between selling price per unit and variable cost per unit.

■ Illustration

How to apply contribution

Stanley Harold Ltd sells each golf ball set for £18. The variable cost is £6 and the early fixed costs are £300,000.

The contribution is therefore

selling price £18 less variable cost £6 = contribution £12

If 60,000 golf ball sets were sold in the year, a statement can be drawn up to show the total contribution and profit for the year.

Statement to show total contribution and profit for Stanley Harold Ltd for the year ended 31 January 2013

	£
Revenue (sales) (60,000 × £18)	1,080,000
Variable costs (60,000 × £6)	(360,000)
Total contribution	720,000
Fixed costs	300,000
Profit for the year	420,000

Fig. 10.2 *Statement to show total contribution and profit*

Break-even analysis

One of the marginal costing techniques is break-even analysis, which identifies the level of output necessary to make neither a profit nor a loss. The break-even point is where total revenue equals total costs.

The number of units required to be sold at the break-even point is calculated using the formula:

$$\frac{\text{total fixed costs}}{\text{contribution per unit}}$$

At the **break-even point**, total revenue equals total cost. There are two methods of calculating this amount:

1 break-even in units × selling price
2 contribution to revenue (sales):

$$\frac{\text{total fixed costs}}{\text{total contribution/revenue (sales)}}$$

■ Illustration

How to apply a formula to calculate the break-even point

Using information from the previous illustration for Stanley Harold Ltd:

■ the selling price for each golf ball set is £18
■ the variable cost per set is £6
■ the fixed costs for the year are £300,000.

The break-even point is therefore

$$\frac{\text{fixed costs}}{\text{contribution per unit}} = \frac{£300,000}{£12} = 25,000 \text{ golf ball sets}$$

The revenue at break-even is the same as total costs. In the above example this can therefore be calculated as

break-even in units × selling price = 25,000 × £18 = £450,000.

Alternatively, using the contribution to revenue (sales) method,

$$\frac{\text{fixed costs}}{\text{contribution per unit/selling price per unit}} = \frac{£300,000}{£12/£18} = £450,000$$

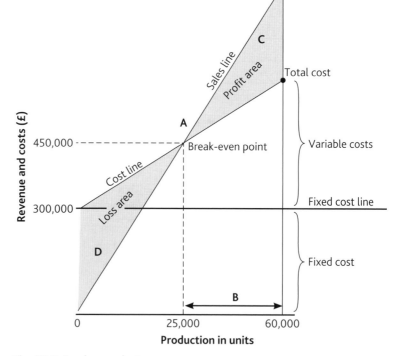

Fig. 10.3 *Break-even chart*

To draw a break-even chart the steps are as follows:

1 Label the axes clearly.
2 Calculate the break-even point using the formula:

$$\frac{\text{total fixed costs}}{\text{contribution per unit}}$$

3 Calculate the break-even point in revenue using the formula:
break-even point in units × selling price per unit

4 Plot the break-even point on the chart (point A). Try to ensure that the break-even sales units and sales revenue are in the middle of the chart.

5 Draw the fixed costs line across the chart as a horizontal line.

6 Draw the sale revenue line starting from (0,0) and going through the break-even point (point A).

7 Draw the total cost line starting from the point where the fixed cost line crosses the y-axis and going through the break-even point (point A).

8 Complete the chart by identifying the profit and loss areas and the margin of safety (line B).

The chart can be used to graphically illustrate:

■ the break-even point where total costs cross total revenues

■ the margin of safety being the difference between the break-even point and the maximum output production level; this is usually expressed in units

■ profit or loss at various production levels being the difference between the total costs and the total revenues lines at different production levels. On the chart, loss area = D and profit area = C.

Margin of safety

The **margin of safety** is the amount of units between the amount of revenue (sales) made and the amount needed to break-even, where the amount of revenue (sales) exceeds the break-even point.

In the previous example Stanley Harold Ltd has a margin of safety of 60,000 − 25,000 = 35,000 golf ball sets. This means that it is making profit on the sales of 35,000 golf ball sets, namely 58.33% of its total revenue (sales). The rest is used to cover the fixed costs.

Target profit

The break-even formula can also be slightly amended to find the units required to be sold to achieve a specified target profit:

$$\frac{\text{total fixed costs} + \text{target profit}}{\text{contribution per unit}}$$

Activity

2 Draw a break-even chart with the following information:

■ selling price of £40 per unit
■ variable cost of £25 per unit
■ fixed costs of £60,000 per year.

Identify the break-even point, the areas of profit and loss and the margin of safety.

Key term

Margin of safety: the difference between the number of sales units achieved (or maximum output) and the number of units at the break-even point, where the amount of sales achieved must exceed the break-even point otherwise a loss is made.

Illustration

How to calculate the units that need to be sold to achieve a target profit

The directors of Stanley Harold Ltd wish to achieve a target profit level of £36,000.

The golf ball sets they would have to produce and sell would therefore be

$$\frac{\text{total fixed costs} + \text{target profit}}{\text{contribution per unit}} = \frac{£300,000 + £36,000}{£12} = 28,000 \text{ golf ball sets}$$

Break-even chart

This information can all be represented on a break-even chart, i.e. a diagram showing where budgeted production exceeds the break-even point and so profit is made.

Limitations of break-even analysis

There are various limitations of break-even analysis:

- It assumes that there are no changes in the levels of inventory so everything produced during that period is assumed to have been sold. This is unrealistic as most businesses have changing levels of inventory throughout the financial year.

- It does not allow product mix and is usually calculated for a single product, which is not realistic.

- Cost behaviour is assumed to be either fixed or variable, so semi-variable costs are not considered. Again this is unrealistic as many costs have behaviour that is not either perfectly fixed or perfectly variable but a combination of the two.

- Fixed costs are assumed to remain fixed for the whole period of time, so stepped fixed costs are not considered. Stepped fixed costs are costs that remain fixed until a certain level of business activity is reached, when they increase in increments. They will remain fixed at this new increment until the next level of business activity. For example an increase in the storage costs due to an increase in the production level.

- Variable costs are assumed to be perfectly linear with the level of production, so changes in costs are not considered, for example overtime or bulk-buying discounts.

- The selling price is assumed to remain fixed throughout the year, so seasonal sales or discounts are again not considered.

Applying marginal costing in decision-making situations

Marginal costing can be used in a variety of business situations:

- whether to make or buy the products
- whether to accept a special order
- how to maximise profits where there are limited resources available.

Make or buy situations

One of the most common business decisions is whether a business should continue to manufacture the products themselves or whether to buy the products in from a supplier. Often the business is faced with a choice of satisfying customer demand with inventory bought in as it is unable to produce the goods required itself. On a purely financial basis the decision whether to make or buy in should be based on whether a positive contribution is made.

■ Illustration

How to reach make-or-buy decisions

Stanley Harold Ltd has six machines that are used in the manufacture of the golf ball sets. One of the machines has broken down and will take four weeks to repair. While the machine is being repaired the directors can lease a replacement machine which would cost £3,000 per week. The staff will need to be trained at a cost of £4,000 to use the machine, which would reduce production in that week from 5,000 golf ball sets to 4,000. Alternatively the directors can buy the golf ball sets in from a competitor at cost of £8 per set. The company would be able to buy 5,000 a week but would also have to pay a fixed delivery cost of £1,275.

The profit for this machine under both options for the four weeks would be as shown below.

	To manufacture	To buy in
	£	£
Revenue		
– to manufacture (4,000 × 1 wk + 5,000 × 3 wks) × £18	342,000	
– to buy in (5,000 × 4 wks) × £18		360,000
Variable costs of materials and labour (4,000 × 1 + 5,000 × 3) × £6	(114,000)	
Buy-in cost (5,000 × 4) × £8		(160,000)
Lease (4 × £3,000)	(12,000)	
Delivery costs		(1,275)
Training costs	(4,000)	
Profit	212,000	198,725

Fig. 10.4 *Profit comparison between manufacturing 19,000 golf ball sets and buying in 20,000 golf ball sets*

Explanatory notes

- The procedure is to again identify the behaviour of each cost and revenue, that is to identify whether a cost varies with the level of production or does not vary with production and is therefore fixed. In this illustration the revenue, variable costs of materials and labour and buy-in costs are variable. The lease, training costs and delivery costs are fixed.

- The illustration shows that the business makes more profit from manufacturing the golf ball sets themselves despite the extra lease and training costs and reduction in revenue. The recommended action would be to continue to manufacture the golf ball sets themselves in order to maximise profit.

Special orders

Before accepting a special order the business must consider both the financial and non-financial factors. Financially it is important as to whether the order provides a positive contribution or not. But non-financial factors are important too, for example whether the order will lead to further orders and expand their share of the market, whether spare capacity is being utilised, will staff have to be retrained to make the product and will they wish to be retrained, will machinery have to be adapted if the specification of the product has been changed, how reliable is the customer, and how much disruption to the normal trading of the business will take place?

Illustration

How to evaluate a special order

Stanley Harold Ltd currently manufactures 60,000 golf ball sets a year but has spare capacity. The company receives a new order for 500 golf ball sets at £12 per set. The customer is based overseas in a new market area. There will be extra packaging costs for the order of £550, which is £1.10 per golf set.

The contribution for each golf ball set in the new order is shown below.

	£
Selling price	12.00
Variable manufacturing costs	(6.00)
Extra packaging costs	(1.10)
Contribution	4.90

Fig. 10.5 *Contribution*

Show the skills

When making a decision on whether to recommend acceptance of a special order you should consider both the financial and non-financial factors to give a balanced answer. Then a judgement should be made that can be for or against as long as it is justified.

Although this contribution is lower than the usual contribution of £12, the new order does make a positive contribution. The business has already passed the break-even point and is producing more units than is required for the target profit. It has spare capacity and therefore any extra contribution will be pure profit.

The total profit from this order will therefore be $500 \times £4.90 = £2,450$.

The non-financial factors should also be considered, namely that the order has been received from a new customer in a new overseas market area, which will expand Stanley Harold Ltd's customer base. However, how reliable is this new customer? Can they guarantee that the new customer will pay on time? Also how easy will the distribution of the products be to the new customer?

Once these factors have been considered to the satisfaction of the business managers then the order should be accepted as it will increase profit as there is a positive contribution.

Limiting factors

A business will often manufacture multiple products but have limited resources available to do so, for example limited labour hours or limited machine hours. An optimum production plan has to be devised in order to maximise profit with the resources available.

The process is as follows.

1 Calculate the contribution per unit.
2 Calculate the contribution per limiting factor, for example per labour hour.
3 Rank the products in order of the product with the highest contribution per limiting factor down to the product with the lowest.
4 Devise a production plan to maximise profits using the rank order.

Illustration

How to devise an optimum production plan

The directors of Stanley Harold Ltd decide to introduce a new product. They intend to manufacture and sell boxes of golf tees.

Information on their two products is as follows.

Table 1 *Information*

	Box of golf tees	Set of golf balls
Selling price	£6	£18
Labour	10 minutes at £3.60 per hour	30 minutes at £8.00 per hour
Materials	£1.80	£2
Expected demand for the following year	24,000 boxes	60,000 sets

The company only has 32,000 hours available and wishes to maximise profits by devising an optimum production plan.

- The contribution per unit (selling price per unit less variable cost per unit) is

  box of golf tees: £6 – £2.40 = £3.60
  set of golf balls: £18 – £6 = £12

- The contribution per limiting factor (contribution per unit divided by proportion of labour hours per unit) is

  box of golf tees: $\dfrac{£3.60}{^1/_6} = £22.50$

  set of golf balls: $\dfrac{£12}{^1/_2} = £24$

- The rank order based on the highest contribution per limiting factor is therefore

  set of golf balls: number 1
  box of golf tees: number 2

- The optimum production plan to maximise profit is therefore as follows.

Table 2 *Plan*

	Units	Hours
Sets of golf balls (expected demand)	60,000 sets requiring 30 minutes per box	30,000
Boxes of golf tees (remaining hours)	12,000 boxes requiring 10 minutes per set	2,000

Explanatory note

The amount of boxes of golf tees to be produced is based on the amount of remaining hours. There are 2,000 hours remaining. Each box takes 10 minutes to produce, and there are 60 minutes in an hour so six boxes can be produced in one hour, making a final calculation of 2,000 hours × 6 = 12,000 boxes.

In this chapter you will have learnt:

- how to explain the method of marginal costing

- how to explain the cost behaviour of direct costs, indirect costs, variable costs, fixed costs and semi-variable costs

- how to explain the terms 'contribution' and 'break-even'

- how to calculate the break-even point in units and revenue using the formulae

- how to represent the break-even point on a chart

- how to explain the limitations of break-even analysis

- how to select and apply marginal-costing techniques for decision-making on make-or-buy decisions, special orders, and the maximisation of profit by finding the optimum production plan with a limiting factor.

Practice questions

1   AQA ACC4 June 2005 (adapted)

The following break-even graph relates to Bungay Books Ltd for the year ending 31 December 2013.

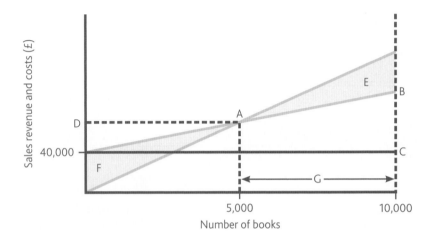

The selling price is £15 per book.

Required

(a)   Identify each of the following shown in the graph.

    A

    Line B

    Line C

    D

    Area E

    Area F

    G.

(b)   Calculate the value indicated at point D on the graph.

(c)   Calculate the marginal cost per unit.

(d)   Calculate the contribution per unit.

(e)   Calculate the profit if 7,200 books are sold. Use your contribution per unit calculated in part (d).

2   Kelsa Ltd manufactures units. The manager calculates the selling price based on the following formula:

direct cost per unit × 40%

The costs per unit are:

direct materials 4 metres @ £5.25 per metre

direct labour 1.5 hours @ £12 per hour

The business receives an order for 350 units.

(a)   Calculate the selling price per unit

(b)   Calculate the total price of the order.

3   AQA ACC4 June 2004 (adapted)

Tom owns a business that manufactures kettles at a marginal cost of £18 each.

The selling price is £22.50 per kettle.

The fixed costs are currently £90,000 per annum.

Required

(a)   Explain the term 'marginal cost'. Give an example.

(b)   Calculate the break-even point in units and revenue.

(c)   Calculate the total contribution if 25,000 kettles are sold.

(d)   Identify the formula used to calculate the profit for the year margin.

(e)   Calculate the profit for the year to sales margin if 25,000 kettles are sold.

(f)   Calculate how many extra kettles will need to be sold if the fixed costs increase next year by 20%.

(g)   Calculate the selling price per kettle if the same profit for the year margin is required after the increase in fixed costs. (Assume that 25,000 kettles will be sold.)

(h)   Draft a memorandum addressed to Tom explaining one advantage and one disadvantage of using break-even analysis.

> **Link**
>
> For further information on the profit for the year margin, see *AQA Accounting AS*, Chapter 9.

4   AQA ACC4 January 2008

Sid owns a business in a seaside resort. He sells greetings cards.

On average each card costs 50p to buy and is sold for £1.20.

The annual business fixed costs are £110,000.

Sid has set a target profit for the year of £30,000.

Required

(a)   Calculate the contribution per greetings card.

(b)   Calculate the number of greetings cards that Sid needs to sell to achieve the target profit of £30,000. State the formula used.

Unfortunately, Sid's supplier decides to increase the cost of the greetings cards by 30%.

Required

(c)   Calculate the number of *extra* greetings cards that Sid would need to sell to maintain a target profit of £30,000 following the increase in cost per card.

Sid does not believe that the business can sell the *extra* greetings cards in the seaside resort.

Required

(d)   Advise Sid of *two* methods by which the business could maintain profit levels without selling the extra greetings cards.

5   Samson Ltd produces gym equipment.

Currently the manufacturing cost for a set of weights is: materials £14, labour £8.

The selling price of each set of weights is calculated as direct cost plus a mark-up of 40%. This selling price remains fixed for all customers.

The company is working at full capacity but has a cash flow problem as some of the clients are taking up to 45 days to settle their accounts.

The manager has received an order of 400 sets of weights from a new customer who is willing to pay cash on delivery. In order to complete this order overtime would have to be paid at an extra cost of £4 per set.

Alternatively the business can purchase the sets from an overseas supplier at a cost of £28 per set. However, there would also be a delivery charge of £600 for the order.

Explain whether Samson Ltd should manufacture the sets of weights by paying overtime or whether the sets should be purchased from the overseas supplier.

6   AQA ACC7 June 2002 (adapted)

Gifton Ltd manufactures only two products, Alpha and Beta.

At present, the factory has one machine that is operating at 100% capacity. Only 520,000 labour hours are available in the year.

The cost per unit is as follows.

	Alpha	Beta
Direct materials	10 metres at £5 per metre	20 metres at £5 per metre
Direct labour	44 hours at £5 per hour	32 hours at £5 per hour

The fixed costs for the year are £440,000.

The selling prices for one unit of Alpha and Beta are £390 and £350 respectively.

Demand in units for the year are as follows.

	Alpha units	Beta units
Gifton Ltd	18,000	8,000

At present Gifton Ltd sells to 40% of the Beta market and 80% of the Alpha market.

Required

(a)   Calculate the contribution per unit for each product.

(b)   (i)   Calculate the contribution per labour hour per unit for each product.

(ii) State the optimum production plan that Gifton Ltd could introduce which would maximise profit.

(c)   Assess the effects this new production plan would have on the manufacturing companies in competition with Gifton Ltd.

7   Cilin Ltd manufactures two products, the Qi and the Xi.

The Xi currently has a selling price of £30 per unit and costs £22 to manufacture (direct materials £8 and direct labour £14).

The Qi currently has a selling price of £20 per unit and it costs £15 to manufacture (direct materials £5 and direct labour £10).

Forty thousand units of Xi and 18,000 units of Qi are usually sold each year.

The Xi is selling well but the economic climate has led to a decrease in the number of units of Qi sold (to 14,000) and the financial manager of Cilin Ltd is unsure whether to reduce the selling price down to £18 to try to meet competitors' prices or whether to buy the products in, partly completed. These products could be bought in at a cost of £12 each and each unit would need to be completed at an extra cost of £2. Unfortunately these products have a lower quality than the ones produced by Cilin Ltd and if purchased, over 40% of the workforce would need to be made redundant.

Discuss whether Cilin Ltd should make or buy in the product Qi.

11 Absorption costing

In this chapter you will learn how to:

- explain the term 'absorption costing'
- calculate profit using absorption costing
- explain the term 'cost centre'
- allocate and apportion costs
- calculate overhead absorption rates
- apply overhead absorption rates
- apply concepts to pricing policy
- cost a simple project.

Key terms

Cost unit: a unit of production or service that absorbs the cost centre's overheads costs, for example a product such as a television set or a service such as a restaurant meal.

Allocation: the process of charging costs which derive from a cost centre directly to that particular cost centre.

Apportionment: the process of charging overhead costs to a cost centre on a rational basis.

Cost centre: a production or service location whose costs may be attributed to cost units, for example a production department.

Production department: where the product is actually made, for example the machining department.

Labour intensive: the production or service location has more direct labour hours than machine hours.

In the previous chapter you were introduced to one of the most commonly used methods in cost accounting, namely marginal costing. However, this method is often compared to the use of another method of cost accounting, namely absorption costing. The main difference between the two is the treatment of fixed costs, which is covered within this chapter. Do not dismiss either method as both methods have their own uses and limitations.

Case study

Maureen Rose plc

Maureen Rose plc manufactures bags. The company has one factory. There are two production departments: cutting and finishing, and two service departments: maintenance and canteen.

Absorption costing

Absorption costing absorbs the factory overheads into the total production cost for each **cost unit** produced in a factory. Whereas marginal costing only considers the variable costs, absorption costing considers all production costs including fixed and variable overheads.

The process of absorption occurs when all production overheads are **allocated** and **apportioned** to a **cost centre**, which is a location such as a **production department**. The total is then absorbed into a cost unit, such as a product or service, using an overhead absorption rate (OAR).

The methods of absorption include:

- direct labour hour rate
- direct machine hour rate.

The basis selected is based on which factor most influences the overhead, for example if the production department uses mostly labour hours it is described as **labour intensive** and the direct labour hour rate is chosen. If the production department uses mostly machine hours it is described as either **machine intensive** or capital intensive and the direct machine hour rate is chosen.

Calculation of the overhead absorption rate (OAR)

The stages used to calculate the overhead absorption rate are as follows.

1 Distinguish between production departments, for example a cutting department, and service departments, for example the canteen.

2 Decide on the correct bases to be used to apportion the overheads between the departments, for example according to the percentage of the total floor space for the cutting department and the proportion of employees working in the department for the canteen.

Activities

1. List five possible **service departments** that a large manufacturing public limited company could have.

2. List five possible service departments that a school or college could have.

Explanatory notes

See Fig. 11.2

- Bases of apportionment: The basis to be used to apportion the overheads is easily identified as it is usually the most realistic, for example insurance. The most equitable way to apportion the building insurance overhead is by the proportion of floor space held by each department whereas a better way to apportion the machine insurance is according to the proportion of the total machine net book value. Given the information available the most realistic basis to be used for the heating and lighting and rent is the proportion of the total floor space in both instances.

- Apportionment of the service departments: The most important thing to recognise is whether there is any interdependency between the service departments. In this case both service departments support the production departments but the canteen also supports the maintenance department. Once this has been identified then this service department must be apportioned first to both the production departments and the other service department.

3. Draw up a schedule to apportion the overheads between all of the departments.

4. Complete the schedule by apportioning the total of the overheads of each service department to each of the production departments.

5. Total up the overheads for each production department.

6. Divide the total for each department by the correct basis, for example labour hours or machine hours depending on whether the department is labour intensive or machine intensive, to give the overhead absorption rate (OAR) for each production department.

Stages 1–5

Illustration

How to apportion overheads using the elimination method, or simplified method

The following information is available for Maureen Rose plc for the year ended 31 October 2013.

Information available for Maureen Rose plc for the year ended 31 October 2013

	£
Overheads:	
Buildings insurance	50,000
Heating and lighting	70,000
Machine insurance	100,000
Rent	120,000
Cutting supervisor	37,100
Finishing supervisors	76,900

Fig. 11.1 *Information*

Additional information:

Table 1 *Additional information*

	Cutting department	Finishing department	Maintenance	Canteen
Floor area, m²	50,000	30,000	15,000	5,000
Machine net book value	£150,000	£450,000	–	–

The service departments are apportioned to the production departments on the following basis.

Table 2 *Service department apportionment*

	Cutting department	Finishing department	Maintenance	Canteen
	%	%	%	%
Canteen	50	40	10	–
Maintenance	75	25	–	–

The overhead apportionment schedule would therefore appear as follows.

Overhead apportionment schedule for Maureen Rose plc

Overhead	Basis	Cutting	Finishing	Maintenance	Canteen
		£	£	£	£
Cutting supervisor	Direct	37,100	–	–	–
Finishing supervisors	Direct	–	76,900	–	–
Buildings insurance	Floor area	25,000	15,000	7,500	2,500
Heating and lighting	Floor area	35,000	21,000	10,500	3,500
Machine insurance	Machine NBV	25,000	75,000	–	–
Rent	Floor area	60,000	36,000	18,000	6,000
		182,100	223,900	36,000	12,000
Canteen	(50% : 40% : 10%)	6,000	4,800	1,200	(12,000)
Maintenance	(75% : 25%)	27,900	9,300	(37,200)	–
		216,000	238,000	–	–

Fig. 11.2 *Overhead apportionment schedule*

The elimination method of apportioning the reciprocal service departments' overheads is quick, as each service department has its overheads apportioned only once to the other departments. However, if the service department with the apportionment from the other service department is not apportioned first, the continuous allotment method will result. Here there is no preferred order to the apportionment, which continues until the balance in each service department is zero. This is not the recommended method for the examinations due to time constraints.

Illustration

How to apportion overheads using the continous allotment method, or repeated distribution method

Using the information from the previous illustration, we would have the following overhead apportionment schedule.

Study tip

When there is interdependency between the service departments remember to include the first service department apportionment in the second service department apportionment. In the above example remember to include the 10% of the canteen costs in the apportionment of the total maintenance costs.

Overhead	Basis	Cutting	Finishing	Maintenance	Canteen
		£	£	£	£
b/fwd		182,100	223,900	36,000	12,000
Maintenance	(75% : 25%)	27,000	9,000	(36,000)	–
Canteen	(50% : 40% : 10%)	6,000	4,800	1,200	(12,000)
Maintenance	(75% : 25%)	900	300	(1,200)	–
		216,000	238,000	–	–

Fig. 11.3 *Overhead apportionment schedule*

Activity

3 List five different overheads and state a reasonable basis for each one which could be used to apportion the overhead to the different production departments.

Study tip

Make sure that the schedule is clearly laid out with each part of the process clearly shown as marks are allocated for each stage.

Study tip

Ensure that the basis used for each overhead is clearly identified as there are usually marks in the examination for doing this.

Key terms

Overhead absorption rate (OAR): the rate that is used to absorb the overheads into the cost unit. It is calculated as either rate per direct machine hour or rate per direct labour hour depending on which the department uses the most.

Full cost: the production cost of each cost unit and includes both direct and indirect costs.

Show the skills

Always state the overhead absorption rate (OAR) in pounds and pence (that is to two decimal places). A calculation of £16.248 should thus be given as £16.25.

Explanatory note

The total production or full cost can now be calculated by absorbing the overheads according to the amount of machine hours and labour hours used by the cost unit and adding them to the direct costs. Each OAR is applied separately.

As can be seen, the same final answer is achieved but the process is longer. This can be a repetitive process if each department apportions their overheads to each other repeatedly.

Stage 6

Illustration

How to calculate the overhead absorption rate (OAR)

The directors of Maureen Rose plc absorb their overheads on the following basis:

▪ The cutting department uses more direct machine hours than direct labour hours. It is therefore machine or capital intensive and overheads are absorbed using direct machine hours.

▪ The finishing department uses more direct labour hours than direct machine hours. It is therefore labour intensive and overheads are absorbed using direct labour hours.

The overheads for the year ended 31 October 2013 were:

▪ cutting department: £216,000
▪ finishing department: £238,000.

The cutting department has 12,000 machine hours and the finishing department has 14,000 labour hours.

The **overhead absorption rate (OAR)** is the rate at which the overheads are absorbed into the cost unit. It is calculated as

$$\frac{\text{department overhead in pounds}}{\text{department direct machine hours or direct labour hours}}$$

The overhead absorption rate for the cutting department is therefore

$$\frac{£216,000}{£12,000} = £18.00 \text{ per machine hour}$$

The overhead absorption rate for the finishing department is therefore

$$\frac{£238,000}{14,000} = £17.00 \text{ per labour hour}$$

Use of the overhead absorption rate (OAR)

Once the OAR has been calculated it is possible to calculate the **full cost** of a cost unit.

Illustration

How to calculate the full cost of a cost unit

Maureen Rose plc has the following information:

▪ Each bag takes 30 minutes of machine time in the cutting department and 2 hours of labour in the finishing department, at £8 per hour, to manufacture.

▪ Each bag uses 0.5 metres of material at £22 per metre.

The full cost per bag is therefore as shown below.

	£
Materials (0.5 metres × £22 per metre)	11.00
Labour (2 hours × £8 per hour)	16.00
Cutting department overheads (£18.00 per machine hour × 0.5 hours)	9.00
Finishing department overheads (£17.00 per labour hour × 2 hours)	34.00
Full cost	70.00

Fig. 11.4 *Cost per bag*

Pricing strategies

Companies often base their pricing strategy on the budgeted full cost of a cost unit.

For example, if the directors of Maureen Rose plc expect next year's costs to be identical to this year's and also wish to use the pricing strategy, budgeted full cost + 20%, the selling price for the next period would be £70.00 × 1.2 = £84.00.

This naturally assumes that budgeted costs are realistic estimations of the future actual costs.

The profit from each cost unit sold is, therefore, £14.

Under-absorption or over-absorption

Absorption rates are often calculated on budgeted costs and production levels at the start of the year. This can lead to problems when actual costs and volumes of production are not the same as those budgeted, leading to an **under-absorption** or **over-absorption** of costs. The difference between the budgeted overheads and the actual overheads is recorded as an adjustment within the income statement (second section). Under-absorption is when fewer units are produced than was predicted, which means that not all costs have been passed on to the cost unit and therefore profit is less, whereas over-absorption is when more units are produced, which means that more costs have been passed on to the cost unit and therefore profit is more.

◼ Inventory valuation

The different methods of costing give a different cost per unit, which will give a different valuation of the closing inventory of the finished goods and work in progress. This in turn will affect the cost of sale figure and the profit calculation when inventory levels change.

Marginal costing will value inventory at the variable cost but absorption costing will absorb the fixed costs into the inventory valuation. This will give a higher value of closing inventory, which will be carried forward to the next accounting period as opening inventory and so fixed costs can be charged to a period other than the one in which they were incurred.

Illustration

Inventory valuation and the effect on profit

Maureen Rose plc has the following information for each bag at 31 October 2013:

	£
Selling price per bag	100.50
Materials per bag	11.00
Labour per bag	16.00
Cutting dept overheads	27.00
Finishing dept overheads	29.75

- The marginal cost per bag is therefore £27.00 (11.00 + 16.00) and the full absorption cost per bag is £83.75 (27.00 + 27.00 + 29.75).
- During the year ended 31 October 2013 the business produced 8,000 bags and sold 7,900 bags.
- Inventory levels were:

	Number of bags
1 November 2012	800
31 October 2013	900

Fixed costs for the year were £454,000.

The comparative income statements for the year ended 31 October 2013 will appear as follows:

	Marginal Costing	Absorption Costing
	£	£
Revenue from sales (7,900 × 100.50)	793,950	793,950
Opening inventory (800 × 27/83.75)	21,600	67,000
Cost of production (8,000 × 27/83.75)	216,000	670,000
Closing inventory (900 × 27/83.75)	24,300	75,375
Contribution	**580,650**	
Fixed costs	454,000	
Profit	**126,650**	**132,325**

The profits are identical whichever method is used when there is no change in inventory levels. However, when the inventory levels change between the start and end of the year, the inventory valuation has an impact on profit.

The additional profit of £5,675 by using the absorption system is due to £5,675 of the fixed costs being absorbed into the closing inventory and effectively carried into the next year.

Therefore the differences in reported profits are only timing differences – the differences in profit are simply reported in different accounting years.

In this chapter you will have learnt:

- how to explain absorption costing to distinguish it from marginal costing
- how to distinguish between a cost centre and a cost unit
- how to allocate, apportion and absorb overheads using the absorption rate
- how to apply the absorption rates to work out the full cost of a cost unit, and from there to work out the selling price of a product.

Practice questions

1. (a) Distinguish between the terms 'allocation', 'apportion' and 'absorption'.

   (b) Explain the terms 'cost centre' and 'cost unit'.

2. AQA ACC7 June 2002 (adapted)

   The following information relates to the production departments of Swanson Ltd:

	Cutting department	Machining department
Direct machine hours	14,000	32,000
Direct labour hours	20,000	20,000
Cost of machinery	20,000	260,000
Floor area (m²)	9,000	21,000

   The factory overheads for the year ended 31 March 2013 were:

	£
Machinery insurance	28,000
Rent	67,000
Machinery depreciation	42,000
Light and heat	28,000

   (a) Prepare an overhead apportionment schedule apportioning the factory overheads to the appropriate departments.

   (b) Calculate the overhead absorption rates for each production department. State the bases used and give one reason for your choice.

   (c) Explain how the OAR could be used by the manager of Swanson Ltd.

3. A company manufactures several products, one of which is the Danthea. The factory has two production centres: Machining and Finishing, and one service centre: the canteen. Eighty per cent of the canteen costs are apportioned to the machining department and the rest to the finishing department. The overheads for the year were:

	£
Machining	208,000
Finishing	72,000
Canteen	40,000

   The following information is available for one unit of Danthea:

Direct materials	£42
Machining department	5 direct labour hours
Finishing department	2 direct labour hours

   Indirect costs are absorbed from the production departments using a direct labour rate.

   Direct labour hours for the year were: Machining department 120,000 hours; Finishing department 25,000 hours.

   All direct labour is paid at £8.00 an hour.

   (a) Calculate the OAR for each production department.

   (b) Calculate the full cost of one Danthea.

Explanatory note

In the illustration the production run costs of one unit of Noc is five times that of one unit of Ein. This arose as the product Noc has fewer production runs than the product Ein. The cost of each product therefore varies according to the product's level of activity. This difference would not be identified using the absorption costing method where the cost of production runs is treated as part of general overheads.

It can therefore be seen that more activity causes more costs to be incurred. If an order requires six requisitions then six times the cost of issuing rate is allocated to that order. Activity-based costing therefore directly links the activity with the costs.

Illustration

How to use activity-based costing in the manufacturing sector

Einnoc Ltd has identified a major activity as the production runs of the factory machines. The cost pool associated with this activity in a financial year is expected to be £500,000. The cost driver of this activity is the number of runs, as the costs increase in direct proportion to this number. A batch of either product requires one production run. It is expected that there will be 50 production runs in the financial year.

The cost driver rate is £500,000/50 = £10,000 per production run.

Using this rate one unit of Ein would incur production run costs of £10,000/1,000 = £10 and one unit of Noc would incur production run costs of £10,000/200 = £50. These production run costs are then added to the other unit costs to calculate the total production cost per unit.

Comparisons between the different methods of costing

Table 2 *Costing methods*

	Marginal costing	Absorption costing	Activity-based costing
Uses	For decision making, as it identifies the extra costs and revenues incurred by the production and sale of an additional unit, e.g. make-or-buy decisions, limiting factors, break-even analysis.	For decision making, as it includes a portion of fixed costs into each cost unit, e.g. calculating the selling price using the pricing strategy 'full cost plus'.	For decision making, as it charges each product with an accurate cost based on its use of an activity. If the activity changes, the related effect on the cost can be assessed, so costs can be controlled. For example, how much will costs increase if there is an extra batch run?
Benefits	Easily understood and applied in decision making, being cost effective. Contribution is identified, which is useful, e.g. in make-or-buy decisions and where there are limiting factors such as limited labour hours.	All costs are considered, so a total production cost per unit is identified. The effect of an increase in any one cost can be assessed, whether it is direct or indirect.	Avoids apportioning overheads using a basis that may not be relevant, e.g. machine hours for administration costs. Batch sizes influence costs, which is ignored by absorption costing, e.g. set-up costs are more expensive for small production runs.
Limitations	Indirect and direct costs are both divided into either fixed or variable costs. Fixed costs are not allocated to cost centres and cost units, but are regarded as time-based and are linked to accounting periods rather than units of output.	The final basis used to calculate the overhead absorption rate may not be relevant for all the overheads in the production department. New technology has led to a reduction in the use of labour hours as a valid basis. If inventory levels decrease, absorption costing records a lower profit as costs from previous periods are set against income.	There are still cost pools that are not caused by one particular cost driver but by several, e.g. the cost of marketing is caused by the number of staff hours and the number of marketing campaigns.

Activity

1 Identify five business activities, their cost pools and a cost driver for each activity. Select at least two activities from the service sector.

In this chapter you will have learnt:

- the term 'activity-based costing'
- how to explain and identify cost pools and cost drivers
- how to compare the uses of activity-based costing against both marginal and absorption costing, while identifying the fact that each method has its own benefits and limitations.

Practice questions

1 Define the term 'activity-based costing'.

2 Explain the terms 'cost pool' and 'cost driver'. Give an example of each.

3 Define each of the following terms:
   - activity-based costing
   - marginal costing
   - absorption costing.

   Explain one benefit and one limitation of using each method to set the selling price of a product.

4 'Activity-based costing was developed as an alternative to absorption costing.'
   (a) Explain how activity-based costing is used to calculate the cost of a product.
   (b) Explain *two* benefits of using activity-based costing as opposed to using absorption costing.

5 Cao plc produces a variety of products according to customer demand. Some products have had the same specification for many years whereas others are regularly updated to meet customer requirements. Some products have long production runs while others are produced in small batches for specific customers.

   Write a memorandum to the financial director of Cao plc explaining whether marginal costing, absorption costing or activity-based costing would be the most appropriate costing method for the company.

6 AQA ACC4 January 2011
   'The idea behind this method of costing is that it is the cause of a cost which is important and not whether it is fixed or variable.'
   (a) Identify the costing method described in the above quotation.
   (b) Explain the advantages of a costing method that is focused on the cause of a cost.
   (c) Identify a business that could use this costing method.

13 Standard costing and variance analysis

One of the major uses of any costing information is the evaluation of performance. Not only calculating how much each product has cost to make but also evaluating how much it **should** have cost to make. The first was discussed in the previous three chapters and now the last will be covered in this chapter, when we look at standard costing. Once a business has set standard or expected costs it can then compare them to actual costs and evaluate its performance either as a whole or department by department. Obviously if costs are more than they should have been then actions need to be taken so that the reasons behind these increased costs can be investigated, so profit is not reduced in the future. The same comparison can also be made between standard revenues and actual revenues. In this chapter you will be introduced to standard costing and the performance decisions that can be made using standard costs and revenues.

Topic 1   Standard costing

In this topic you will learn how to:

- explain the term 'standard costing'
- explain how standard costs are determined
- evaluate standard costing.

Key terms

Standard costing: the preparation and use of standard costs, including the calculation of variances.

Standard cost: a predetermined cost that should be achieved through an efficient working environment.

Case study

Legin Ltd

Legin Ltd manufactures a single product, the Keza. For many years the financial director has maintained a standard costing system.

What is standard costing?

Standard costing is the preparation and use of costs that should be achieved with efficient working conditions and manufacturing performance. These costs ought to be achieved and are called **standard costs**. Standard costing involves the comparison of these predetermined standard costs with actual costs. Any difference between the actual and standard cost is called a variance, and should be investigated.

Illustration

How to calculate standard costs

The financial director of Legin Ltd has calculated the standard costs per unit of Keza as follows.

	£
Direct materials (4 metres at £5 per metre)	20.00
Direct labour (6 hours at £8 per hour)	48.00
Standard cost per unit	68.00

Fig. 13.1 *Standard cost card per unit of Keza*

The purposes of standard costing

Standard costing is frequently used within a manufacturing business as it provides detailed information to management which helps to establish why budgeted performance differs from actual performance.

Its many purposes include:

- assisting in budget setting and evaluating performance
- acting as a control device by highlighting those activities that are not performing as expected and may need investigation and corrective action
- providing information on future costs for future decision-making
- providing a motivating target for employees to aim for
- providing an acceptable cost for valuing inventory.

Setting standards

Standards must be achievable as they are a yardstick against which efficiency is measured. If based on ideal working conditions, where the workers and machines are working to optimum efficiency at all times, the standards will be demotivating as they will never be achieved. Similarly, if based on a basic fixed standard that has been in force for many years and can be easily achieved due to advances in technology, the standards can be equally demotivating. Therefore they should be a realistic target by allowing for eventualities such as staff sickness and machine breakdown.

- Standards are usually based on past performance. This is the most cost-effective method, but there may be past inefficiencies that would then be built into the future standards.
- Standards can also be set using engineering studies where workers are observed using time and motion studies. However, again these can be misleading as well as costly to establish as they take time to complete and workers may not give a realistic impression of their normal working performance as they may feel that they will be judged on it. Working too quickly would set too high standards which cannot be achieved and working too slowly may result in dismissal.

Sources of information for setting standards for direct costs

The following are examples of sources of information for setting standards for direct costs. It is not an exhaustive list.

Direct material

Amount of material used:

- observation of the manufacturing process
- records of historical amounts used
- technical data from the supplier on recommended amounts to be used
- product specification
- past data on the amount of wastage
- an assessment of the quality of the material to be used
- an assessment of the performance of the equipment and labour force available.

Explanatory note

The **standard cost card** on p138 shows that each unit of Keza should use 4 metres of material that cost £5 per metre and 6 hours of labour that cost £8 per hour. In total £20 should be spent on material and £48 on labour.

Key term

Standard cost card: specifies the standard costs predetermined for one unit.

Cost of material:

- predicted currency exchange rates
- price list from suppliers including any bulk buying, trade or cash discounts available
- information on predicted inflation
- records of historical costs paid
- data on the effects on cost of anticipated seasonal variations/scarce availability.

Direct labour

Amount of labour time:

- an assessment of the training and skills of the workforce
- an assessment of any changes in production processes
- observation of the workforce, for example by time and motion studies
- records of historical output and efficiency levels.

Cost of labour:

- data on current pay rates after considering the grade of workforce used
- data on industry and local rates
- published legislation, for example on the minimum wage
- an assessment of any anticipated wage rises and bonuses
- an assessment of future overtime rates.

Advantages and disadvantages of standard costing

Advantages

- Predetermined standards make the preparation of forecasts and budgets much easier as the information has already been collected.
- Costs and revenues are controlled through the use of variances, that is the comparison of standard costs with actual results, which will highlight the efficiencies and inefficiencies within the business. Remedial actions can then be taken.
- The recording of inventory issues is simplified as they are all at standard cost.
- Both internal and external reports can then be produced from the standard costing bookkeeping system.
- Employees can be motivated to achieve targets, which should result in better performance especially if rewards are given when targets are achieved or passed.

Disadvantages

- Standards have little use if set either too high or too low, and so must be regularly reviewed and reset.
- Standards are best used for businesses that have a well-established and repetitive process so that resetting of standards is kept to a minimum.
- Collecting the information to set a standard may be time-consuming and costly.
- In a rapidly changing technological economy the information may quickly become out of date.

Activity

1 List three different products in a new manufacturing business, in an established manufacturing business and in the service industry. Describe the different measures that would have to be taken to collate the necessary information needed to draw up the cost standards for each.

In this topic you will have learnt:

- the term 'standard costing'
- how standard costs are predetermined
- the advantages and disadvantages of using standard costing.

Practice questions

1   Define the term 'standard cost'.

2   Explain *two* advantages and *two* disadvantages of using standard costing to a manufacturing business.

3   Evaluate the different methods by which standards can be set.

Topic 2   Variance analysis

In this topic you will learn how to:

■ calculate variances and sub-variances

■ explain the significance of each variance and sub-variance, including interrelationships between variances

■ explain how businesses use variances and sub-variances

■ prepare statements reconciling budgeted profit with actual profit based on variances

■ prepare statements reconciling budgeted costs with actual costs based on variances.

Key terms

Variance: the difference between a standard cost or revenue and an actual cost or revenue.

Favourable variance: the actual figures are better than the standard figures in the budget resulting in a higher actual profit than was expected.

Adverse variance: the actual figures are worse than the standard figures in the budget, resulting in a lower actual profit than was expected.

Cost variance: the difference between the standard cost and the actual cost.

What is variance analysis?

Variance analysis is the process of comparing actual costs and revenues with standard costs and revenues and investigating any reasons for the difference between them. Corrective action can then be taken by each budget manager. This is known as management by exception.

Variances are categorised into either a **favourable variance** or an **adverse variance**.

A favourable variance has a positive effect on profit, that is, the actual costs are lower than the standard, or actual revenue is higher than the standard.

An adverse variance has a negative effect on profit, that is, the actual costs are higher than the standard, or actual revenue is lower than the standard.

A manager will usually look into the possible causes of an adverse variance as this decreases profit. A favourable variance will increase profit, but if there is a large favourable variance it may still need to be investigated as it could be as a result of poor budget setting. Remember that if budgets are easily achieved they lose validity as targets.

Variances and sub-variances

The following variances are to be studied for the examination:

■ Material total **cost variance**: the difference between the standard expected cost and the actual cost of material.

■ Labour total cost variance: the difference between the standard expected cost and the actual cost of labour.

■ Sales (revenue) total variance: the difference between the standard revenue expected and the actual revenue received from units (sold).

Each total variance is broken down into two **sub-variances** so fuller analysis can be made of the reasons for the variance. Namely did the variance arise due to a difference in prices paid or due to a difference in the resources used?

■ Material total cost variance: price sub-variance and usage sub-variance

■ Labour total cost variance: rate sub-variance and efficiency sub-variance

■ Sales (revenue) total variance: price sub-variance and volume sub-variance.

Illustration

How to calculate labour cost variance

The labour total cost variance for Legin Ltd is as follows.

	£	
Standard cost (4,000 × £48.00)	192,000	
Actual cost (4,000 × £45.00)	180,000	
Total cost variance	12,000	favourable

Fig. 13.7 *Labour cost variance*

Labour rate variance

The actual number of hours used to produce 4,000 units was 5 hours × 4,000 = 20,000 hours.

	£	
Standard cost should have been (20,000 × £8)	160,000	
Actual cost was (20,000 × £9)	180,000	
Labour rate variance	20,000	adverse

Fig. 13.8 *Labour rate variance*

Labour efficiency variance

The standard quantity of labour for 4,000 units was expected to be 6 hours × 4,000 = 24,000 hours.

	£	
Standard efficiency should have been (24,000 × £8)	192,000	
Actual efficiency was (20,000 × £8)	160,000	
Labour efficiency variance	32,000	favourable

Fig. 13.9 *Labour efficiency variance*

The calculations of the sub-variances can be checked:

£32,000 favourable – £20,000 adverse = £12,000 favourable total variance

Alternative method of variance calculation

Some students find it easier to calculate the sub-variances using formulae. This tends to be quicker.

Illustration

How to calculate variances using formulae

Using the information from the previous illustrations, the variances can be calculated as follows.

- *Material price variance*:

    actual quantity of material AQ(actual price paid per metre AP – standard price paid per metre SP) = AQ(AP – SP)

    The variance is therefore calculated as 14,000(£6 – £5) = £14,000 adverse.

- *Material usage variance*:

    standard price paid SP(actual quantity of material used AQ – standard quantity of material SQ) = SP(AQ – SQ)

    The variance is therefore calculated as £5(14,000 – 16,000) = £10,000 favourable.

- *Labour rate variance*:

    actual amount of hours AH(actual rate paid per hour AR – standard rate paid per hour SR) = AH(AR – SR)

    The variance is therefore calculated as 20,000(£9 – £8) = £20,000 adverse.

- *Labour efficiency variance*:

    standard rate paid SR(actual amount of hours AH – standard amount of hours SH) = SR(AH – SH)

    The variance is therefore calculated as £8(20,000 – 24,000) = £32,000 favourable.

This illustration shows that the results are the same whichever method is used. In the examination it does not matter which method is used.

Interrelationship between cost variances

Often the cost variances may be interlinked by a common cause. The reason for one sub-variance can lead to the occurrence of another sub-variance. This is called an interrelationship. In the case study there are two possible interrelationships between the two variances:

- The material is of better quality so the labour force wastes less and therefore appears more efficient.
- The labour is more skilled so the material is not wasted and therefore there is better material usage.

Possible reasons for the cost variances

If we assume that the standard costs are based on reasonable and achievable budgets and are not either ideal standards or basic standards that are out of date, then there are many other reasons which could explain how variances arise. The following is a list of some of the possible causes of variances.

Explanatory notes

- It can therefore be seen that the £12,000 favourable variance is split between the two sub-variances.
- The adverse labour rate variance means that the workforce was paid more per hour than was expected, whereas the favourable efficiency variance shows that the workforce was more efficient than was expected and produced the goods in fewer hours.
- One possible reason for these variances is that the workforce was more skilled and therefore was able to command a higher rate per hour but at the same time was able to be more efficient with its time.
- Of the two variances the adverse rate variance should be investigated to see whether Legin Ltd can employ a cheaper workforce paying less per hour but with the same skills. Labour could perhaps be brought in from overseas which may be cheaper. The large favourable efficiency variance should also be checked as it may be as a result of overestimating the time needed for the production of one unit.

Study tip

In the examination, marks are not just awarded for the calculation of the variance. Always state the variance with both a pound sign and the direction, that is, whether the variance is adverse or favourable. There are marks in the examination for the direction and marks could also be lost if a pound sign is not given.

Table 1 *Causes of cost variances*

Variance	Direction	Explanation	Cause
Material price	Adverse	More paid for the material per metre/ kilogram	Higher price charged by supplier
			Unexpected delivery costs
			Better-quality materials
			No bulk discounts
			Scarcity of materials
	Favourable	Less paid for the material per metre/ kilogram	Lower price charged by supplier
			Lower-quality materials
			Unexpected trade/cash discounts
Material usage	Adverse	More materials used for production	Lower-quality material
			Theft, obsolescence, deterioration
			Less-skilled workforce
	Favourable	Fewer materials used for production	More skilled/efficient workforce
			Efficient production processes
			Higher-quality material
Labour rate	Adverse	More paid per hour to the workforce	Unexpected overtime
			Productivity bonuses
			Trade union action
			Rise in minimum wage rates
			Better-skilled workforce
	Favourable	Less paid per hour to the workforce	Lower-grade workforce
			No overtime or bonuses
Labour efficiency	Adverse	More hours used for production	Lower-skilled workforce
			Lower quality of materials
			Unfavourable working conditions
			Lack of training
			Lack of supervision
			Works to rule/strikes (if paid)
			Machine breakdowns
			Lack of materials/orders
			Too many unproductive hours, e.g. coffee breaks
	Favourable	Fewer hours used for production	More-skilled workforce
			Better-quality material
			Fewer non-productive hours
			More training/supervision
			Advances in machine technology

Cost reconciliation

Variances are often used by management to analyse the change in total costs for a period. Budgeted costs are reconciled to actual costs.

▪ Illustration

How to prepare a cost reconciliation statement

The budgeted costs for Legin Ltd for month 1 were as follows.

	£
Direct materials (£20 × 4,000)	80,000
Direct labour (£48 × 4,000)	192,000
Budgeted costs	272,000

Fig. 13.10 *Budgeted costs*

The actual costs for Legin Ltd for month 1 were as shown below.

	£
Direct materials (£21 × 4,000)	84,000
Direct labour (£45 × 4,000)	180,000
Actual costs	264,000

Fig. 13.11 *Actual costs*

A cost reconciliation for month 1 for Legin Ltd would therefore be drawn up as follows.

Cost reconciliation statement for Legin Ltd for month 1

	£ADV	£FAV	£
Budgeted costs (4,000 × £68)			272,000
Material price variance	14,000		
Material usage variance		10,000	
Total variance			4,000
Labour rate variance	20,000		
Labour efficiency variance		32,000	
Total variance			(12,000)
Actual cost (4,000 × £66)			264,000

Fig. 13.12 *Cost reconciliation statement*

Sales (revenue) variances

As well as cost sub-variances it is possible to calculate sub-variances for revenue, that is differences in sales price and sales volume.

▪ Explanatory notes

- This illustration shows that there has been a reduction in total cost which can be split into the four different sub-variances.
- The overall reduction in total cost is £8,000, which can be checked as (£68 – £66) × 4,000.

▪ Key term

Sales (revenue) variance: the difference between the standard revenue and actual revenue.

Explanatory note

As there had been a reduction in costs and no change in the level of fixed overheads, then a possible reason for the drop in profit could be a reduction in the amount of revenue for the month. Had less been sold or had there been a reduction in the selling price? The revenue (sales) sub-variances can be calculated and analysed to provide possible answers for these questions.

Study tip

A common mistake in the examination is for the direction of sales (revenue) variances to be misstated. In summary it is the opposite to cost variances, if the actual revenue is less than the standard revenue then it is adverse as profit is reduced, and vice versa for a favourable variance.

Key terms

Sales price variance: the difference between the actual selling price per product and the standard selling price expected per product, for the actual units sold.

Sales volume variance: the difference between the actual number of units sold and the standard number of units expected to be sold, at the standard selling price.

Illustration

How to calculate and analyse a sales (revenue) variance

In month 1 the financial director of Legin Ltd was concerned to notice that despite a reduction in costs the total profit had decreased. He provides the following additional information for the month.

- The expected sales for that month were 3,800 units at £90 each.
- Fixed overheads for the month were expected to be £50,000.
- Profit was expected to be £20,000.
- The actual sales for the month were 3,900 units at £85 each.
- There were no changes in the level of fixed overheads.

Illustration

How to calculate sales (revenue) variances

The total sales (revenue) variance is as follows.

	£	
Standard revenue (3,800 × £90)	342,000	
Actual revenue (3,900 × £85)	331,500	
Sales (revenue) total variance	10,500	adverse

Fig. 13.13 *Sales (revenue) total variance*

This illustration shows that there is a reduction in revenue which will reduce profit and therefore needs to be investigated.

The **sales price variance** is shown below.

	£	
Standard revenue should have been (3,900 × £90)	351,000	
Actual revenue was (3,900 × £85)	331,500	
Sales price variance	19,500	adverse

Fig. 13.14 *Sales price variance*

The **sales volume variance** is as follows.

	£	
Standard revenue volume should have been (3,800 × £90)	342,000	
Actual revenue volume was (3,900 × £90)	351,000	
Sales volume variance	9,000	favourable

Fig. 13.15 *Sales volume variance*

The calculations of the sub-variances can be checked:

£19,500 adverse – £9,000 favourable = £10,500 adverse total variance

Alternative method of sales (revenue) variance calculation by formulae

These variances can also be calculated using formulae.

■ Illustration

How to calculate sales (revenue) variances using formulae

Using the information from the previous illustration, we have the following.

▨ Sales price variance:
actual sales units AS(actual selling price ASP – standard selling price SSP) = AS(ASP – ASS)
The variance is therefore calculated as £3,900(£85 – £90) = £19,500 adverse.

▨ Sales volume variance:
standard selling price SSP(actual sales units AS – standard sales units SS) = SSP(AS – SS)
The variance can therefore be calculated as £90(3,900 – 3,800) = £9,000 favourable.

■ Explanatory notes

■ Fig. 13.15 shows that although there is a total adverse variance of £10,500 which reduces profit, there is a favourable element: the business has actually sold more units than it expected, as shown by the favourable sales volume variance.

■ This, however, was achieved by reducing the price, which resulted in an adverse sales price variance.

■ The business needs to investigate whether an increase in sales volume can only be achieved through reducing price. Perhaps there is increased competition and the business has no choice.

Possible reasons for sales (revenue) variances

Table 2 *Causes of sales (revenue) variances*

Variance	Direction	Explanation	Cause
Sales price	Adverse	Actual selling price is lower than expected	Responding to change in fashion
			Responding to increased competition
			Responding to lack of demand
			Reduced quality of product
			Pricing strategy, e.g. price penetration
	Favourable	Actual selling price is higher than expected	Action as market leader
			Lack of competition
			Increased quality increases demand
			Price-creaming pricing strategy used
			Start of product life cycle
Sales volume	Adverse	Actual level of sales units is lower than expected	Changes in trends and fashion
			Loss of market share
			End of product life cycle, so market saturated
			Lack of demand due to lower quality
	Favourable	Actual level of sales units is higher than expected	Change in trends and fashion
			Higher quality increases demand
			Lack of supply by competitors

Profit reconciliation

All of these variances can be used to produce a profit reconciliation that reconciles budgeted profit with actual profit.

 Illustration

How to prepare a profit reconciliation statement

The budgeted profit for Legin Ltd for month 1 was as follows.

	£
Budgeted revenue (3,800 × £90)	342,000
Budgeted direct costs	(272,000)
Budgeted fixed costs	(50,000)
Budgeted profit	20,000

Fig. 13.16 *Budgeted profit*

The actual profit for Legin Ltd for month 1 was as follows.

	£
Actual revenue (3,900 × £85)	331,500
Actual direct costs	(264,000)
Actual fixed costs	(50,000)
Actual profit	17,500

Fig. 13.17 *Actual profit*

A profit reconciliation for Legin Ltd for month 1 would therefore be drawn up as follows.

Profit reconciliation statement for Legin Ltd for month 1

	£
Budgeted profit	20,000
Sales price variance	(19,500)
Sales volume variance	9,000
Cost variances	8,000
Actual profit	17,500

Fig. 13.18 *Profit reconciliation statement*

> **Explanatory note**
>
> The actual profit for the month has reduced by £2,500 when compared to the budgeted profit. A reconciliation statement can be drawn up which summarises the reasons for this reduction; namely despite the reduction in costs during the month the increase in the number of goods sold did not cover the loss in profit due to a lower selling price. The net effect was a reduction in profit.

Flexing the budget

Unfortunately the budgeted production levels are not always the same as the actual production levels. It is of no use to compare costs at one level of production with the costs at another level of production. Cost patterns vary according to the levels of activity. These variances would make no sense. It is then necessary to **flex the budgeted figures** so that like-with-like comparisons can be made.

> **Key term**
>
> **Flexed budget:** amending standard costs for changes in levels of production.

Illustration

How to flex a budget

Flexed approach to variances

The production in month 2 was 4,500 units.

The actual costs for month 2 were as follows.

	£
Direct materials (14,400 metres of material were used)	86,400
Direct labour (20,250 hours of labour were used)	182,250

Fig. 13.19 *Actual costs*

Total material variance

The total material variance was as follows.

	£	
Standard cost (4,500 × £20)	90,000	
Actual cost	86,400	
Total material variance	3,600	favourable

Fig. 13.20 *Total material variance*

Material price

The price per metre is calculated as $\dfrac{£86,400}{14,400} = £6$.

	£	
Standard cost should have been (14,400 × £5)	72,000	
Actual cost (14,400 × £6)	86,400	
Material price variance	14,400	adverse

Fig. 13.21 *Material price variance*

However, as the production levels are different the material usage variance must be flexed.

Therefore the standard expected usage of material for the actual production level is 4 metres per unit × actual production of 4,500 units = 18,000 metres.

Material usage variance

The material usage variance is as follows.

	£	
Standard usage for actual production (4,500 × 4 × £5)	90,000	
Actual usage (14,400 × £5)	72,000	
Material usage variance	18,000	favourable

Fig. 13.22 *Material usage variance*

Explanatory note

The standard cost is calculated using the actual production level of 4,500 so that costs can be compared using like-with-like. It is of limited use comparing costs at one level of production with the costs at another level of production as it is expected that they will be different.

Explanatory note

Again the actual quantity of material is used within the calculation of standard cost so that comparisons of like-with-like can be made. What is the difference between actual costs with that quantity of material and the expected standard costs for the same quantity of material?

Explanatory note

The standard usage is again calculated using the actual level of production so comparisons can be made with the actual usage for this level of production. What is the difference between actual usage of material and the expected standard usage for the same level of production?

Explanatory note

Even when using the formulae the material usage variance must be flexed as actual production differs from budgeted production. (The standard amount of material that was expected to be used at this level of production must be calculated.)

The calculations of the sub-variances can be checked:

£18,000 favourable – £14,400 adverse = £3,600 favourable total variance

Alternatively, using the formulae

The material price variance is AQ(AP – SP):

14,400(£6 – £5) = £14,400 adverse

The material usage variance is SP(AQ – SQF), where SQF stands for the standard quantity of material flexed for actual production:

£5(14,400 – 18,000) = £18,000 favourable

Total labour variance

The total labour variance was as follows.

	£	
Standard cost (4,500 × £48)	216,000	
Actual cost	182,250	
Total labour variance	33,750	favourable

Fig. 13.23 *Total labour variance*

Labour rate variance

The rate per hour is calculated as $\dfrac{£182,250}{20,250} = £9$.

	£	
Standard cost (20,250 × £8)	162,000	
Actual cost (20,250 × £9)	182,250	
Labour rate variance	20,250	adverse

Fig. 13.24 *Labour rate variance*

However, as the production levels are different again the labour efficiency variance must be flexed.

Therefore the standard expected efficiency of labour at the actual production level is

6 hours per unit × actual production of 4,500 units = 27,000 hours

Labour efficiency variance

The labour efficiency variance is as follows.

	£	
Standard efficiency at actual production (27,000 × £8)	216,000	
Actual efficiency (20,250 × £8)	162,000	
Labour efficiency variance	54,000	favourable

Fig. 13.25 *Labour efficiency variance*

> **Explanatory note**
>
> Once again the standard cost is calculated using the actual production level of 4,500 so that actual costs at one level of production can be compared to the standard costs at the same level of production.

> **Explanatory note**
>
> Again the actual amount of labour hours is used within the calculation of standard cost. What is the difference between actual costs with that amount of hours and the expected standard costs for the same amount of hours?

> **Explanatory note**
>
> The standard efficiency is again calculated using the actual level of production so comparisons can be made with the actual efficiency for this level of production. What is the difference between actual efficiency of labour and the expected standard efficiency for the same level of production?

> **Explanatory note**
>
> Even when using the formulae the labour efficiency variance must be flexed as actual production differs from budgeted production. (The standard amount of labour hours that was expected to be used at this level of production must be calculated.)

The calculations of sub-variances can be checked:

£54,000 favourable – £20,250 adverse = £33,750 favourable total variance

Alternatively, using the formulae

The labour rate variance is AH(AR – SR):

20,250 (£9 – £8) = £20,250 adverse

The labour efficiency variance is SR(AH – SHF), where SHF stands for standard hours of labour flexed for actual production:

£8(20,250 – 27,000) = £54,000 favourable

The topic of variance analysis is a common examination question that many candidates find difficult. It is recommended that strategies are developed to remember the calculation methods, for example devising a personal mnemonic. However, just as important as the calculations are the reasons for these variances, the reconciliations and methods that a business would use to improve results.

Cost reconciliation when production levels are different

In month 2 the amount of production was different to the amount expected. In a cost reconciliation an amendment has to be made to the budgeted cost, namely the budgeted cost for actual production has to be reconciled with the actual cost for actual production.

Cost reconciliation statement for Legin Ltd for month 2

	£ADV	£FAV	£
Budgeted costs (4,500 × £68)			306,000
Material price variance	14,400		
Material usage variance		18,000	
Total variance			(3,600)
Labour rate variance	20,250		
Labour efficiency variance		54,000	
Total variance			(33,750)
Actual cost (86,400 + 182,250)			268,650

Fig. 13.26 *Cost reconciliation statement for month 2*

The reconciliation should reconcile the budgeted costs with the actual costs at the same level of production. In other words it should compare like with like. The only amendment to the cost reconciliation from the procedure used in Fig. 13.12 is to change the budgeted costs for actual production levels.

In this topic you will have learnt:

- how to calculate the total material, labour and sales (revenue) variances and their respective sub-variances
- how to calculate the variances with a flexed budget
- the significance of each variance, including the interrelationships between them
- the meaning of each variance and how businesses use variances
- how to prepare statements reconciling budgeted profit with actual profit and budgeted costs with actual costs.

Practice questions

1   Define the term variance. Assess the usefulness of calculating variances when evaluating the performance of a business.

2   Explain why budgets must be flexed when preparing some variances.

3   AQA ACC7 January 2003 (adapted)

The budgeted profit for Handley Enterprises Ltd for the year ended 31 October 2013 is £61,500. Bob, the management accountant, has calculated the following variances for that year.

	£	
Materials price	2,000	adverse
Materials usage	500	favourable
Labour rate	4,000	adverse
Labour efficiency	1,000	favourable

There are no other variances.

Required

(a)   State one possible cause of each of the above variances and explain any possible interrelationship between them. Identify which variances Bob should investigate.

(b)   Calculate the actual profit for the year ended 31 October 2013.

4   AQA ACC7 January 2005 (adapted)

Kirill Ltd manufactures one product.

The following variances have been calculated for the year ended 31 December 2013.

	£	
Material price	1,400	adverse
Material usage	600	favourable
Labour rate	2,400	favourable
Labour efficiency	900	adverse
Sales price	1,800	adverse
Sales volume	200	favourable

The budgeted total cost was £124,600.

(a)   Calculate the actual total cost for the year ended 31 December 2013.

(b)   Explain the effect of all the variances on profit. Which variances should be investigated and why?

5   AQA ACC7 June 2002 (adapted)

Hall plc manufactures a single product.

The budgeted costs per unit for the month March 2013 were as follows.

	£
Direct materials (£4 per metre)	8.00
Direct labour (£10 per hour)	22.50

The anticipated production for March was 20,000 units.

The actual results for March were as follows.

	£
Materials (40,000 metres)	140,000
Labour (45,000 hours)	405,000

The actual costs were based on the production of 18,500 units.

Required

(a)   Calculate:

(i)   the material price and usage sub-variances

(ii)   the labour rate and efficiency sub-variances.

(b)   Explain why these sub-variances may have occurred.

(c)   Prepare a cost reconciliation for the month of March 2013, reconciling total budgeted costs with actual costs.

6   AQA ACC7 June 2008 (adapted)

Spencer Ltd manufactures a single product, the Spenz.

The following information relates to the month of May 2013.

	Budgeted	Actual
Production	2,400 units	2,200 units
Direct material	5 kilos at £5.50 per kilo per unit	£66,000 (13,200 kilos)
Direct labour	6 hours at £4.50 per hour per unit	£70,400 (17,600 hours)

The budgeted profit for May 2013 was £26,000.

Required

(a)   Calculate the material price and material usage sub-variances.

(b)   Calculate the labour rate and labour efficiency sub-variances.

(c)   Calculate the actual profit for Spencer Ltd for the month ended May 2013.

(d)   Explain two possible ways in which the variances will affect the current workforce.

7   Thea sells horse blankets.

For the year ending 31 August 2013 she expected to sell 2,500 blankets at £40 each.

Each blanket is expected to cost £22. This is made up of 1.5 metres of material at £10 a metre and 30 minutes to make the blanket at £14 an hour.

Her actual results for the year were 2,700 blankets were sold for £102,600.

To make the blankets she used 4,320 metres of material costing £34,560 and 2,025 hours of labour costing £24,300.

(a)   Calculate the total sales (revenue) variance and the sales price and sales volume sub-variances.

(b)   Calculate the total material variance and the material price and material usage sub-variances.

(c)   Calculate the total labour variance and the labour rate and labour efficiency sub-variances.

(d)   Calculate the expected profit for the year ending 31 August 2013 and reconcile it with the actual profit for the year.

(e)   Explain to Thea why her actual profit is different to the expected profit and make recommendations on how she can improve her profitability.

14 Capital investment appraisal

One of the most important decisions that a business will make is whether or not to invest money on a capital item, for example the purchase of a new factory. This expenditure will decrease their liquidity in the short term but must be beneficial in the long term. In this chapter you will learn the techniques used to assess whether an investment of a capital nature should be undertaken from a financial point of view. At the same time in examination questions you would be expected to also consider non-financial consequences of the investment. The topic is called capital investment appraisal.

Topic 1 Payback

In this topic you will learn how to:

- explain what is meant by capital investment and a capital investment appraisal
- explain the concept of payback
- calculate cash inflows, cash outflows and net cash inflows and so make calculations using the payback method of capital investment appraisal
- evaluate the payback method.

Key terms

Capital investment appraisal: the process of using cash flows to decide whether a capital project should be undertaken.

Payback: a calculation of how long it takes to generate enough cash inflows to cover the initial cost of a capital project.

Case study

Jacklyn Ltd

Jacklyn Ltd has manufactured a single product for many years. One of the production machines needs replacing at a cost of £80,000.

What is meant by capital investment appraisal?

Capital investment appraisal is the process of calculating future cash flows of a capital project, for example the purchase of a new machine or capital investment in the development of a new product, in order to make a decision as to whether the capital project should be undertaken.

Two methods of capital investment appraisal are considered:

- payback
- net present value.

Payback

Payback is the time it takes for the cash inflow generated by a capital project to equal the cash outflow. More simply it is the length of time that is required for the net cash inflows to cover the cost of investment. The shorter the payback period the better. This is especially important if the business has cash-flow problems or will have to borrow the money for the capital project as the inflows can first be used to reduce the loan and then can be used for other potentially income earning purposes.

Illustration

How to calculate payback time

The machine is expected to last four years. The financial director of Jacklyn Ltd has calculated the expected cash flows for the new machine as follows.

Explanatory note

It is important to show the workings for all stages in case of addition errors. Cumulative net cash inflows are the net cash inflow of one year added to the cumulative net cash inflow of the previous year. They need only be calculated up to the year nearest the cost of investment, in the illustration this is year 2.

Show the skills

Be careful about how you state your answers on payback. Do not round up so much that the answer is inaccurate. The usual practice is to round up to two decimal places. If the answer is given in days round up to the nearest day.

Study tip

Make sure that if the examination question asks for the payback period to be stated in a certain format, then you answer in that format, for example in years and days.

Study tip

Beware of depreciation. A common error in the examination is for candidates to include depreciation as a cash outflow. This is not correct, as depreciation does not involve the movement of cash.

Activity

1 Discuss in pairs the reasons why some businesses need a quick payback period.

	Inflows	Outflows
	£	£
Year 1	50,000	15,000
Year 2	70,000	35,000
Year 3	80,000	40,000
Year 4	90,000	40,000

Fig. 14.1 *Cash flows*

The cash inflows are from the sale of the manufactured goods, whereas the cash outflows are all the production costs, excluding depreciation as this is does not involve the movement of cash.

	Net cash inflows	Cumulative net cash inflows
	£	£
Year 1	35,000	35,000
Year 2 (A)	35,000	70,000 (B)
Year 3	40,000 (C)	110,000
Year 4	50,000	160,000

Fig. 14.2 *Cash inflows and outflows*

At the end of year 2 the cumulative net cash inflow was £70,000. Only another £10,000 is needed to cover the cost of the replaced production machine. The payback period is therefore somewhere between the end of year 2 and the end of year 3.

The payback is therefore calculated as:

year with cumulative net cash inflow nearest cost of investment

$$+ \frac{(\text{cost of investment} - \text{cumulative net cash inflow nearest year})}{(\text{net cash inflow of next year})}$$

$\times$ 365 days/52 weeks/12 months

or

$$A + \frac{(\text{cost of investment} - B)}{C} \times 365 \text{ days/52 weeks/12 months}$$

If the payback for this machine is calculated in years and months, it is therefore

$$2 \text{ years} + \frac{(80,000 - 70,000)}{40,000} \times 12 \text{ months} = 2 \text{ years and 3 months}$$

It therefore takes two years and three months to make enough net cash inflows to cover the initial cost of the investment of £80,000. Once this period has passed, the business has covered its capital costs.

Note: The answer can also be written in years and days, or years and weeks.

For this illustration, the answer would therefore be two years and 91.25 days, or two years and 13 weeks.

Advantages and disadvantages of using the payback method of capital investment appraisal

Advantages

▨ Payback is easy to calculate, understand and is widely used.

▨ The method is used by many businesses as need for quick cash flow has grown in importance in recent years. It should be remembered that a small manufacturer is unlikely to want to wait long for payback whereas a large organisation can perhaps wait a little longer as it may have better access to cash flow or more reasonable rates of borrowing.

Disadvantages

▨ Payback ignores the **time value of money**, that is, £3,000 received today does not have the same purchasing value as £3,000 received in three years' time.

▨ The method ignores the money made after the payback date, for example very little money could be made after the payback date or alternatively considerable money is made after payback. But neither of these possibilities is considered.

▨ It ignores the whole life of the capital project. The project may last a long time after the payback date during which time large cash inflows are received and/or large outflows are paid out, for example expensive repairs or updating of the capital project. These net cash inflows are ignored, so that a capital project that makes significant net cash inflows over the long term is rejected in favour of a capital project with a quicker payback but which only makes net cash inflows over the short term and quickly needs replacing with another capital project.

> **■ Key term**
>
> **Time value of money:** this concept states that money received or paid out in the future does not have the same value as money today.

In this topic you will have learnt:

■ the terms 'capital investment appraisal' and 'payback'

■ how to make calculations using the payback method

■ how to evaluate the payback method, stating its advantages and disadvantages as a means of capital investment appraisal.

Practice questions

1 Explain the term 'payback' and give two possible reasons why a business would be interested in a quick payback period.

2 AQA ACC7 January 2003 (adapted)

Sid Standon Ltd is considering the purchase of either machine E100 or machine F100. The following information applies to these machines.

	E100	F100
	£	£
Purchase price	400,000	500,000
Net cash inflows:		
Year 1	140,000	60,000
Year 2	140,000	120,000
Year 3	140,000	180,000
Year 4	140,000	240,000
Year 5	140,000	300,000

Both machines are expected to be sold after five years, after being depreciated using the straight-line method.

The machine E100 creates toxic waste. This waste would be disposed of using lorries that would travel through the local town.

Required

(a) Calculate the payback period for each machine in years and days.

(b) Which machine would you recommend that Sid Standon Ltd should purchase? Justify your recommendation.

3 Peter runs a shop providing an ironing service. He needs to replace its steam machine.

The ironing service currently irons 80 shirts, 60 blouses and 50 other items a day. Peter charges £2 for a shirt and £2.50 for a blouse. All other items are £1 each. The ironing service operates six days a week, 50 weeks a year.

Peter can buy a new steam machine at a cost of £66,000 with an annual maintenance charge of £2,000. The machine is expected to last five years and will increase the daily output. The number of ironed shirts will increase to 100 a day and blouses to 70 a day. The number of other items will remain the same.

Or alternatively for £13,000 a year he can rent a machine that is similar to his current machine and will not increase output.

Peter pays his three workers £50 each a day. His overheads are £820 a week. Peter pays himself £25,000 a year.

(a) Calculate the annual cash flows from buying the machine.

(b) Calculate the payback period of the steam machine.

(c) Explain whether Peter should buy or rent the steam machine.

Topic 2   Net present value

In order to make a meaningful comparison between today's original cost of a capital project and its future net cash inflows, it is necessary to discount the cash inflows back to the present so that they are equivalent in value to a cash inflow now. This enables a like-with-like comparison to be made. The discount factor is called the **cost of capital**, and it is usually based on the weighted average cost of capital available to the business; that is, the average cost that is needed to raise the required amount of capital to fund the project.

Illustration

How to calculate cost of capital

Jacklyn Ltd has the following capital structure.

		Rate of return	Cost of capital
	£	%	£
Ordinary shares (currently paying a dividend of 12%)	500,000	12	60,000
5% preference shares	200,000	5	10,000
	700,000		70,000

Fig. 14.3 *Capital structure*

The average cost of capital is therefore

$$\frac{\text{cost of capital per annum}}{\text{value of capital}} = \frac{\pounds 70,000}{\pounds 70,000} = 10\%$$

The **net present value** is therefore the sum of the net cash inflows (future cash inflows less future cash outflows after each has been discounted back to the present) less the initial cost of the investment.

- If the net present value's answer is positive then the investment could to be undertaken on purely financial grounds. If there is a choice of capital projects then the one with the highest positive net present value should be considered on financial grounds.

- If the net present value's answer is negative then the investment should be rejected on financial grounds as it means that the sum of future net cash inflows does not cover the initial cost of the investment.

Note: Before a decision can be made whether to undertake an investment all factors need to be considered, that is both financial and non-financial aspects. For example, a capital project may yield a high positive net present value but it creates excessive pollution, which would create bad publicity for the business adversely affecting revenue, so the decision may be made to invest in the capital project with the lower net present value which does not create excessive pollution.

In this topic you will learn how to:

- explain the concept of net present value

- calculate cash inflows, cash outflows and net cash inflows so that net present value can be calculated

- interpret the results of net present value calculations

- evaluate the net present value method of capital investment appraisal

- write a report on a capital investment appraisal using the payback method and the net present value method, including reference to social accounting factors.

Key terms

Cost of capital: the discounting factor used in capital investment appraisals to discount future cash inflows so that they are equivalent in value to cash now.

Net present value: a capital investment appraisal method that uses the present value of net cash inflows to ascertain whether the capital project should be undertaken on financial grounds.

Explanatory note

This illustration explains how a business establishes its cost of capital.

Illustration

How to calculate net present value

In the case study on Jacklyn Ltd, the net cash inflows were calculated as follows.

	£
Year 1	35,000
Year 2	35,000
Year 3	40,000
Year 4	50,000

Fig. 14.4 *Net cash inflows*

The new machine will cost £80,000.

Additional information:

There is a cost of capital of 10%. This means that it will cost Jacklyn Ltd £8,000 (10% of the £80,000) to raise the capital to fund the new machine.

The discount factors are as follows.

	Discount factor
Year 1	0.909
Year 2	0.826
Year 3	0.751
Year 4	0.683

Fig. 14.5 *Discount factors*

Year	Net cash inflow	×	Discount factor	=	Present value
	£				£
0	(80,000)		1.000		(80,000)
1	35,000		0.909		31,815
2	35,000		0.826		28,910
3	40,000		0.751		30,040
4	50,000		0.683		34,150
	80,000			Net present value:	44,915

Fig. 14.6 *Statement to calculate net present value of machine*

■ **Explanatory notes**

■ In year 0, the discount factor is 1 as there has been no passage of time so there is no change in the value of money.

■ In year 1, the discount factor is 0.909 as a year has passed. The net cash inflow of £35,000 is multiplied by 0.909 to give a present value of £31,815.

■ This process continues throughout the life of the machine with the discount factor reducing as time passes.

■ At the end of the life of the machine, the total of net cash inflows of £80,000 has a total positive net present value of £44,915. The positive net present value means that from a financial point of view, the machine should be purchased, as the discounted present value of the net cash inflows exceeds the initial cost of the machine. (The minimum acceptable solution is a zero net present value, as this means that there is a balance with the cost of funds.)

Advantages and disadvantages of using net present value as a method of capital investment appraisal

Advantages

■ This method considers the time value of money by using the discount factors.

■ It includes all the net cash inflows from the whole life of the capital project.

Disadvantages

■ It is more complex to calculate than the payback method.

■ It is based around selecting the relevant cost of capital, which may be difficult to determine with any reliability. The higher the cost of capital, the lower the net present value.

■ It should not be considered on its own, for the project may still not be worth investing in due to the social non-financial factors and a slow payback which could outweigh the benefit of the positive net present value.

Writing a report on a potential capital investment

Often a requirement in the examination is to write a report on a potential capital investment project assessing whether the business should invest in the project or not. When evaluating a capital investment project it is expected that the student will give a balanced answer of both the benefits and limitations of investing in the project considering both financial and non-financial factors before making a final recommendation to invest or not.

■ **Illustration**

How to write a report on a potential capital investment project

Additional information:

Jacklyn Ltd will have to borrow the money to pay for the new machine. This debt has to be paid back over three years. It is also expected that the workforce will have to be trained how to use the new machine. The carbon footprint is expected to be larger with this machine.

Report contents should include, among other factors, the following.

■ Link

See Chapter 16, Social accounting.

Show the skills

In all reports there should be an evaluative process, with a balanced view whereby both sides of the argument are given and a final recommendation is made with a summarised justification.

Financial considerations:

- The payback is in a short period of time and before the debt has to be repaid to the bank.
- The training of the workforce will cost time and money.
- There will be finance costs (interest payable) to pay on the debt. Was this included in the outflows? If not it is an extra cost that needs to be considered.
- Borrowing for this machine may reduce the opportunities of borrowing to fund other areas of the business, for example health and safety.
- How long is the machine expected to last or will it need replacing not long after the payback period?
- Can the machine be leased and not purchased. This may be a cheaper option which will mean that there is no need to borrow from the bank which will aid cash flow and stop finance costs (interest payable) being paid, which is dead money.
- The net present value is positive at a cost of capital of 10%.

Non-financial considerations:

- Some of the workforce may feel threatened by the introduction of a new machine and may resist change by not wanting to be retrained.
- Staff may fear being replaced by the machine and may be demotivated by the lack of money put into other areas of the business.
- Staff may be concerned at the lack of liquidity within the business and may be concerned that there will be no future wage rises or productivity bonuses. This will cause a fall in morale.
- How much disruption will there be whilst the machine is being replaced?
- Can the production process continue without the machine being replaced? If not then unless there are cheaper alternative replacement machines, this machine must be purchased.
- Will the increase in carbon footprint result in action by outside pressure groups including government agencies which may distrupt production?

Final recommendation:

The machine appears to have a relatively quick payback and a positive net present value, so if the machine lasts for at least several more years, and if staff can overcome their concerns, it is recommended that the business purchases the machine.

In this topic you will have learnt:

- the term 'net present value'
- how to calculate the expected net cash inflows from a capital project and from these calculate the net present value
- how to interpret the resulting net present value in that, if it is positive, the project should be undertaken from a financial point of view, and if it is negative it should be rejected
- how to evaluate the net present value, stating its advantages and disadvantages as a method of capital investment appraisal
- how to write a report on a capital investment appraisal using net present value and payback, including reference to social accounting.

Practice questions

1 (a) Explain the terms 'net present value', 'payback' and 'cost of capital'.
 (b) Identify the advantages and disadvantages of using:
  (i) the payback method of capital investment appraisal
  (ii) the net present value methods of capital investment appraisal.

2 AQA ACC7 June 2002 (adapted)

The main cutting machine of Wilkinson Ltd needs to be replaced. A replacement machine will cost £400,000, plus a delivery charge of £5,000.

The current machine cuts 50,000 units a year. The number of units cut is expected to be reduced by 10% in year 1 due to the time taken to install the new machine. The number of units cut is expected to increase to 52,000 units for year 2 and year 3 respectively.

Additional information:

▨ The cost of capital is 10%.

▨ The following is an extract from the present value table for £1.

	10%
Year 1	0.909
Year 2	0.826
Year 3	0.751

▨ It is assumed that revenues are received and costs are paid at the end of the year.

▨ Each unit of production costs £8 to manufacture, increasing to £10 in year 2.

▨ Each unit is expected to sell for £15 in years 1 and 2, increasing by 5% in year 3.

▨ It is assumed that everything produced is sold.

Required

(a) Calculate the annual net cash flows for each year, which are expected to result from the purchase of the machine.

(b) Using the expected annual net cash flows, calculate the net present value for the replacement machine.

(c) State whether or not Wilkinson Ltd should purchase the machine. Give one reason for your answer.

3   Use the information from Question 3 on p160.

Peter has concluded that the payback method does not give him enough information and has decided that he needs to calculate the net present value. The cost of capital is 12%. The discount factors at this cost of capital are as follows:

	Discount factor
Year 1	0.893
Year 2	0.797
Year 3	0.712
Year 4	0.636
Year 5	0.567

(a)   Calculate the net present value for the steam machine.

(b)   Reviewing your calculations for payback and net present value, should Peter buy or lease the machine? Give reasons for your choice.

4   AQA ACC7 June 2008 (adapted)

One of the assembly machines at Roberts Ltd needs to be replaced.

A replacement machine will cost £200,000, which is payable on purchase.

The replacement machine is expected to last four years, but will need a complete maintenance check in year 3 at a cost of £50,000.

The existing machine assembles 4,000 units a year. The number of units assembled by the replacement machine is expected to be 25% lower in year 1 than the existing machine due to the time lost during installation and testing. In year 2 it is expected that 4,500 units will be assembled and this will increase by 20% each year compared to the previous year.

The existing machine produces units at a cost of £26 each, whereas the replacement machine will produce units at a cost of £24 each. The selling price is currently £42 per unit but with the improved quality provided by the replacement machine this will increase to £45 per unit. From year 3, it is expected that the cost of manufacture will increase by 25% each year and the selling price will increase by 30% each year compared to the previous year.

The cost of capital is 14%.

The following is an extract from the present value table for £1.

	14%
Year 1	0.877
Year 2	0.769
Year 3	0.675
Year 4	0.592

It is assumed that all units produced are sold.

It is assumed that revenues are received and costs are paid at the end of each year.

The money to purchase the machine will be borrowed.

Required

(a)   Calculate the expected net cash flows for each year, using the replacement machine.

(b)   Calculate the payback period for the replacement machine.

(c)   Calculate the net present value for the replacement machine using the expected net cash flows.

(d)   Compare the two methods of capital investment appraisal.

(e)   State whether the assembly machine should be purchased. Give reasons for your decision.

15   Budgeting

At AS level you were introduced to the principles of budgeting through the use of the cash budget (as described in *AQA Accounting AS*, Chapter 10). You will already understand that a cash budget can give information to the owners and managers of a business so they can make more informed decisions, for example how much money they are expected to have in the bank in three months' time, as well as the expected sources of the money coming into the business and the levels of expenditure. But the cash budget is not the only budget used by a business. There are many others. In this chapter you will learn some of the other types of budget, as well as the benefits and limitations of budgetary control.

Topic 1   Budgetary control

In this topic you will learn how to:

- explain the benefits of budgetary control

- explain the limitations of budgetary control

- evaluate budgetary control.

Key terms

Budget: a financial plan for the future expressed in quantitative terms. It is used to control the use of resources so that the business objectives can be achieved.

Master budget: taken from the functional budgets and consists of a budgeted income statement and forecast statement of financial position (balance sheet).

Budgeting: the preparation of the budgets.

Budget centre: a department or area for which a budget has been set up.

Budgetary control: responsibility to achieve the budget has been delegated to the budget centre managers.

What is budgetary control?

A **budget** is a short-term financial plan of standard costs and revenues prepared for the future to control resources so that the business objectives can be achieved. All functional budgets are used to prepare the **master budget**, which is a budgeted income statement (second section) and forecast statement of financial position (balance sheet). **Budgeting** is the preparation of the budgets for each **budget centre**, and **budgetary control** is when each budget centre manager has responsibility to:

- justifiably use resources
- control costs
- achieve the activities set by the budget in accordance with the business's objectives.

Each manager's performance is then evaluated by comparing actual results against the targets set for the budget centre, so any underachievement can be analysed and any remedial action can be taken.

Benefits of budgeting

The benefits of budgeting fall into the following main categories.

- Control: A budget is a formal authorisation to a budget centre manager of a specified amount to be allocated to specified activities, thereby resources such as cash and labour hours are controlled.
- Planning: By using a budget, the use of resources, for example cash, materials and labour hours, is planned in order to achieve the objectives of the business.
- Communication and coordination: Budgets communicate plans to managers responsible for carrying them out. They also ensure coordination between managers of sub-units so that each is aware of the others' requirements, for example between the stores, production and sales departments.

■ **Link**

See *AQA Accounting AS*, Unit 2, where budgeting is introduced.

■ Motivation: Budgets are often intended to motivate managers to perform in line with organisational objectives. This especially applies if the managers had been included in the drawing up of the budgets, which will then be realistic and achievable, and if there are rewards for achievement of the budget targets.

■ Performance evaluation and monitoring: The performance of managers is often evaluated by reference to budgetary standards. Any variance between the budget and actual results will then be assessed and corrective action taken.

■ Aid to decision-making: If each manager bases their decision-making around their budget then all departmental decisions will relate to the corporate plan and business objectives.

Limitations of budgetary control

The limitations of using budgetary control are as follows.

■ A budget must be produced within the limiting factors that surround the business, for example the amount of market demand for its product; the number of skilled employees available; the availability of material supplies; the space available either as a working area or for storage; the amount of cash or credit facilities available to finance the business.

■ A budget that is unrealistic or unachievable is of limited use and may do more harm than good, especially considering the negative effect it will have on the workforce who will feel that they are underperforming and their productivity may decline further.

■ Likewise a budget must not be set too low as this is also demotivational. This can happen when there is no goal congruence, or agreement, between the objectives of the manager and the objectives of the business. A manager may feel that the budget is to be used to evaluate and judge his or her performance and so may endeavour to set the budget to an easily achievable target, which at the same time may not motivate his or her team.

■ Budgets can restrict activity so that managers are not innovative and fail to take advantage of unexpected opportunities as their actions are too strictly controlled.

■ Through careful control of their budgets throughout the year managers may have a surplus available at the end of the year, but rather than save this surplus they will spend it so their budget will not be reduced next year. So budgets may inadvertently encourage the waste or inefficient use of resources.

In summary, a budget is only as useful as the standards used to set it. If set too high it is unachievable and demotivates the workforce, and if set too low it fails to motivate and can lead to inefficiencies and an unproductive workforce.

Show the skills

Benefits and limitations must be applied with careful note taken as to whether the business provides a service or produces a product.

In this topic you will have learnt:

■ the benefits of budgetary control

■ the limitations of budgetary control

■ how to evaluate budgetary control.

Practice questions

1   Explain the term 'budgetary control'.

2   Explain how setting a budget may restrict the activities of a business.

3   'Departmental managers should be left to their own devices as then they are free to act in an unrestricted manner and so innovation will be achieved.' Discuss.

Topic 2 Preparing and commenting on budgets

In this topic you will learn how to:

- prepare a range of budgets
- prepare a set of forecast financial statements
- evaluate the performance of a business based on budgeted information
- make recommendations as to how the performance of a business, as revealed by a budget, could be improved.

Study tip

All budgets usually have a vertical breakdown of data for each period or month.

Key term

Sales (revenue) budget: a summary of the expected sales units and revenue value for the future.

Case study

Nawor Halls

Nawor Halls owns a business that manufactures a single product, the Conny. The business operates over 13 periods a year. Each period consists of four weeks with five working days in each week. Last year Nawor had a fixed production of 6,000 units per period regardless of the level of sales units, but this year he wants to introduce a system of budgetary control.

Types of budget

The following are types of functional budget:

- **sales (revenue) budget**
- production budget
- purchases budget
- labour budget
- trade receivables budget
- trade payables budget
- cash budget (already covered in *AQA Accounting AS*, Unit 2).

Sales (revenue) budget

The sales (revenue) budget records the amount of units expected to be sold as well as the expected revenue value per period.

■ Illustration

How to prepare a sales (revenue) budget

The following information is available for Nawor Halls for the first four periods of the new year.

	Period 1	Period 2	Period 3	Period 4
Expected sales units	1,200	1,400	1,500	1,400

Fig. 15.1 *Cash flows*

Each unit of Conny sells for £100.

Sales (revenue) budget of Nawor Halls

	Period 1	Period 2	Period 3	Period 4
Sales units	1,200	1,400	1,500	1,400
Revenue value (units × price)	£120,000	£140,000	£150,000	£140,000

Fig. 15.2 *Sales (revenue) budget for Nawor Halls*

This is a forecast predicting what the revenue (sales) will be in the future, perhaps based on previous periods' revenue or from market research.

Production budget

The **production budget** is the key budget as all production costs will be based on the quantities stated within this budget.

■ Illustration

How to prepare a production budget

Nawor Halls maintains closing inventory at a level sufficient to cover eight days of sales units for the next period. However, storage constraints restrict inventory to a maximum of 580 units. It is assumed that revenue accrues evenly within each period. At the start of period 1 there are expected to be 480 units in inventory.

Production budget of Nawor Halls

	Period 1	Period 2	Period 3
	Units	Units	Units
Revenue (sales)	1,200	1,400	1,500
Opening inventory	(480)	(560)	(580)
Closing inventory (restricted)	560	580	560
Production	1,280	1,420	1,480

Fig. 15.3 *Production budget for Nawor Halls for the first three periods*

Explanatory notes

- This budget is in units only and is coordinated with the information from the sales (revenue) budget.

- The closing inventory is equivalent to eight days of next period's sales units. There are 20 days in a period (13 periods a year, each period has four weeks with five days in a week). Closing inventory is therefore calculated as 8/20 × next period's sales units, for example for period 1 closing inventory is calculated as 8/20 × 1,400 = 560. Due to storage restrictions the amount in closing inventory is limited to a maximum of 580 units. The business can therefore be seen in period 2 to be working to maximum capacity.

- The closing inventory of one month becomes the opening inventory of the next month.

- The units of production are calculated as sales units – opening inventory + closing inventory units.

Purchases budget

The **purchases budget** provides information on the cost of materials.

Illustration

How to prepare a purchases budget

Each Conny consists of 2 metres of material, which costs £15 per metre. The material cost per unit is therefore £30.

Purchases budget for Nawor Halls

	Period 1	Period 2	Period 3
Production units	1,280	1,420	1,480
Material cost (£30 × units)	£38,400	£42,600	£44,400

Fig. 15.4 *Purchases budget for Nawor Halls for the first three periods*

Nawor Halls can therefore see from this budget that the cost of purchases is increasing in line with the level of production. Perhaps he should negotiate a bulk-buying discount with the suppliers.

Labour budget

The **labour budget** identifies the amount of labour hours required to produce the levels of production stated in the production budget. The labour budget also helps management plan work patterns, for example shifts, as well as calculating the expected labour costs.

Illustration

How to prepare a labour budget

Each Conny takes two hours in the machining department and three hours in the assembly department.

The workforce is paid £96 for each shift in the machining department and £60 for each shift in the assembly department.

Machinists complete an eight-hour shift and workers in the assembly department complete a six-hour shift.

Key terms

Purchases budget: a calculation of the expected value of purchases of materials based on the production levels as shown by the production budget.

Labour budget: shows the expected amount of labour hours and the resulting cost of labour based on the production budget.

Labour budget for Nawor Halls

		Period 1	Period 2	Period 3
Units produced		1,280	1,420	1,480
Machining department:				
Machining hours (× 2)		2,560 hours	2,840 hours	2,960 hours
Number of eight-hour shifts		320	355	370
Labour cost (machining department)	A	£30,720	£34,080	£35,520
Assembly department:				
Assembly hours (× 3)		3,840 hours	4,260 hours	4,440 hours
Number of six-hour shifts		640	710	740
Labour cost (assembly department)	B	£38,400	£42,600	£44,400
Total labour cost	A + B	£69,120	£76,680	£79,920

Fig. 15.5 *Labour budget for Nawor Halls for the first three periods*

Explanatory notes

■ The budget is coordinated with information from the production budget.

■ Machining department:

   a Each unit spends two hours in the machining department so multiply the number of units produced by two to calculate the total number of hours.

   b Each shift takes eight hours so divide the total number of hours by eight to achieve the number of shifts.

   c Each shift costs £96 in the machining department so multiply the number of shifts by 96 to achieve the total labour cost for the machining department.(A)

■ Assembly department:

   a Each unit spends three hours in the assembly department so multiply the number of units produced by three to calculate the total number of hours.

   b Each shift takes six hours so divide the total number of hours by six to achieve the number of shifts.

   c Each shift costs £60 in the assembly department so multiply the number of shifts by 60 to achieve the total labour cost for the assembly department.(B)

■ Total labour cost for each period: This is calculated by adding A and B together for each period.

■ The labour budget illustrates that if every worker works five shifts a week the maximum number of machinists he needs is in period 3 (370/5 = 74) and the maximum number of assembly workers is also needed in period 3 (740/5 = 148).

Key term

Trade receivables budget: a summary of the expected movement in money owed by the customers to the business.

Trade receivables budget

The **trade receivables budget** identifies the amount of money expected to be owed by customers each period.

Illustration

How to prepare a trade receivables budget

Nawor Halls expects 20% of each period's revenue to be paid in cash. Therefore 80% of each period's revenue will be on credit terms – half of the credit revenue will pay after one period and the other half will pay after two periods. At the start of period 1 there are trade receivables of £80,000 of which half will pay during the first period and the other half will pay in the second period. There was also a debt from two periods before of £45,000 which is expected to be paid in period 1. Of this debt £10,000 is expected to be a bad debt.

Trade receivables budget for Nawor Halls

	Period 1	Period 2	Period 3
	£	£	£
Balance b/f	80,000	91,000	115,000
Credit revenue	96,000	112,000	120,000
Receipts (credit revenue from previous period)	(40,000)	(48,000)	(56,000)
Receipts (credit revenue from two periods before)	(35,000)	(40,000)	(48,000)
Bad debt	(10,000)	–	–
Balance c/f	91,000	115,000	131,000

Fig. 15.6 *Trade receivables budget for Nawor Halls for the first three periods*

Explanatory notes

- This budget is coordinated with the revenue budget.
- Credit revenue (sales): These are calculated as total revenue less 20% (cash receipts). For example in period 1 the total revenue is £120,000 less the cash receipts of £24,000 = £96,000 credit revenue.
- Receipts:
  - a Half of the credit revenue is received after one month and the other half two months later. For example in period 1 the credit revenue is £96,000 of which half will pay in period 2 and the other half in period 3.
  - b In period 1 the receipts from credit revenue are from trade receivables from the previous year, who are one period old and therefore half (£40,000) will be received in period 1 and the other half in period 2.
  - c In period 1 there are also receipts from credit revenue which are from receivables from the previous year who are two periods old and therefore all will be received in period 1. However, an adjustment must be made for £10,000 of this debt which is bad and will not be recovered. The bad debt is recorded separately.
- Balance c/f: The balance c/f is the amount of trade receivables outstanding for the period and is carried forward to the next period and recorded as balance brought forward.
- It can clearly be seen that the amount of trade receivables is increasing, therefore so is the risk of further bad debts. Nawor Halls should try to encourage more cash revenue perhaps by increasing the amount of cash discount.

Key term

Trade payables budget: a summary of the expected movement in money owed by the business to the suppliers.

Trade payables budget

The **trade payables budget** identifies the amount of money owed to suppliers at the end of each period.

Illustration

How to prepare a trade payables budget

Nawor Halls pays for 25% of his purchases by cash. Therefore 75% of each period's purchases are on credit terms. Eighty per cent of the credit purchases are paid after one period and 20% will pay after two periods. At the start of period 1 there are £22,500 of trade payables of which £18,000 will be paid in the first period and the rest will be paid in the second period. There is also an amount owing from two periods before of £4,000 which is expected to be paid in period 1.

Trade payable budget for Nawor Halls

	Period 1	Period 2	Period 3
	£	£	£
Balance b/f	22,500	29,300	33,710
Credit purchases	28,800	31,950	33,300
Payments (credit purchases from previous period)	(18,000)	(23,040)	(25,560)
Payments (credit purchases from two periods before)	(4,000)	(4,500)	(5,760)
Balance c/f	29,300	33,710	35,690

Fig. 15.7 *Trade payables budget for Nawor Halls for the first three periods*

Activity

1 Explain which budgets would be most useful to the following:
- an international bank
- a hotel
- a small laundrette
- a market stall.

Study tip

Previously, synoptic questions have been set on preparing the **forecast financial statements**, as this tests both budgeting and the layout of the financial statements and statement of financial position (balance sheet). Students also have to know about acceptable methods of inventory valuation to complete the income statement (first section). Any selection of these budgets can be made by the examiner. Therefore you must know all of them!

Key term

Forecast financial statements: the forecast income statement and statement of financial position (balance sheet) based on the functional budgets contained within the master budget.

Explanatory notes

- This budget is coordinated with the purchases budget.
- Credit purchases: These are calculated as total purchases less 25% (cash payments). For example, in period 1 the total purchases are £38,400 less the cash payments of £9,600 = £28,800 credit purchases.
- Payments:
  a Eighty per cent of the credit purchases are paid after one month and 20% two months later. For example, in period 1 the credit purchases are £28,800, of which 80% (£23,040) will be paid in period 2 and the 20% (£5,760) in period 3.
  b In period 1, the payments to credit purchases are to trade payables from the previous year, who are one period old, and therefore 80% (£18,000) will be paid in period 1 and 20% (£4,500) in period 2.
  c In period 1, there are also payments to credit purchases that are to trade payables from the previous year who are two periods old and therefore all will be paid in period 1.
- Balance c/f: The balance carried forward is the amount of trade payables outstanding for the period and is carried forward to the next period and recorded as the balance brought forward.
- It can clearly be seen that Nawor Halls owes an increasing amount to his trade payables.

Master budget

Information is taken from all of the functional budgets and a set of forecast financial statements is produced. This is known as the master budget.

■ Illustration

How to prepare the master budget

Nawor Halls wishes to produce a set of forecast financial statements from his functional budgets as a means of evaluating his expected profitability.

Notes:

▦ The standard cost per unit is as follows.

	£
Direct materials	30
Direct labour (24 + 30)	<u>54</u>
	<u>84</u>

Fig. 15.8 *Standard cost per unit*

▦ Inventory will be valued on the basis of the standard cost per unit.

▦ Overheads for the period are expected to be £45,600.

▦ It is assumed that there is no opening or closing inventory of raw materials or work in progress.

Forecast income statement for three periods

	£	£
Revenue (1,200 + 1,400 + 1,500 units) × £100		410,000
Opening inventory (480 units × £84)	40,320	
Cost of production (1,280 + 1,420 + 1,480) × £84*	351,120	
Closing inventory (560 units × £84)	(47,040)	
Cost of sales (cost of goods sold)		(344,400)
Gross profit		65,600
Bad debt	10,000	
Overheads	45,600	
		(55,600)
Profit for the year		<u>10,000</u>

Fig. 15.9 *Forecast income statement for Nawor Halls for the first three periods*

Additional information:

▦ The non-current assets were expected to have a book value of £166,690.

▦ The balance at the bank was expected to be £5,300.

▦ The amount owing on a long-term loan was expected to be £10,000.

▦ The capital brought forward was expected to be £300,000.

▦ The drawings for the period were expected to be £5,660.

■ Explanatory notes

■ Revenue: This is calculated using the information from the sales (revenue) budget. Each period's sales is added together and then multiplied by the selling price or revenue values for three periods added together.

■ Opening inventory: This is calculated using the opening units from period 1 in the production budget. This is then multiplied by the standard cost per unit.

■ Cost of production: This is calculated using the information from the production budget. Each period's production units are added together and then multiplied by the standard cost.

* Alternatively, the cost of production can be calculated as:

materials from the purchases budget: £38,400 + £42,600 + £44,400 = £125,400

plus labour from the labour budget: £69,120 + £76,680 + £79,920 = £225,720

Therefore production cost = 125,400 + 225,720 = 351,120.

■ Closing inventory: This is calculated using the closing inventory of units from period 3 in the production budget. This is then multiplied by the standard cost per unit.

Explanatory notes

- Closing inventory is the amount in the income statement which is calculated by multiplying the closing inventory in period 3 from the production budget by the standard cost.

- Trade receivables is calculated using the trade receivables budgets as the trade receivables from period 2 (half of period 2's credit revenue (sales), £56,000) plus the trade receivables from period 3 (all of period 3's credit revenue (sales), £120,000).

- Trade payables is calculated using the trade payables budget as the trade payables from period 2 (20% of period 2's credit purchases, £6,390) plus the trade payables from period 3 (all of period 3's credit purchases, £33,300).

Statement of financial position (balance sheet) at end of period 3

	£	£
Non-current assets		166,690
Current assets:		
Inventory	47,040	
Trade receivables	131,000	
cash and cash equivalents (bank and cash)	5,300	
	183,340	
Current liabilities:		
Trade payables	(35,690)	
Net current assets		147,650
		314,340
Non-current liabilities:		
Long-term loan		(10,000)
		304,340
Capital b/f		300,000
Profit for the year		10,000
Drawings		(5,660)
		304,340

Fig. 15.10 *Statement of financial position (balance sheet) for Nawor Halls at the end of period 3*

Nawor Halls can see from the forecast financial statements that he does expect to make a profit, albeit a small one. He is expected to have both a positive net current assets and money in the bank (which would be ascertained from a cash budget). He must ensure that he does not increase the level of his drawings too much. He has a considerable amount of trade receivables that needs careful monitoring otherwise he opens himself up to the possibility of bad debts. So it is recommended that he looks into reducing the level of trade receivables.

In this topic you will have learnt:

- how to prepare a range of budgets
- how to prepare a set of forecast financial statements
- how to evaluate the performance of a business on the basis of budgeted information
- how to make recommendations as to how the performance of a business, as revealed by a budget, could be improved.

Practice questions

1   Explain the term 'budget'.

2   Identify a budget that is *not* useful to the following businesses:
    - a school
    - a firm of accountants
    - a leisure complex
    - a high street butcher.

    Give a reason why the budget is not useful.

3   Identify two uses for each of the following budgets:
    - a labour budget
    - a production budget
    - a trade receivables budget.

4   AQA ACC4 June 2008 (adapted)

    Svetlana Omarova owns a business manufacturing drinking mugs.

    The business operates over 13 four-week periods with five working days in each week.

    Previously, Svetlana had fixed production at 18,000 mugs per period, regardless of the level of sales units. This year Svetlana has decided to introduce a system of budgetary control.

    The sales units for the first four periods of this year are expected to be as follows:

	Period 1	Period 2	Period 3	Period 4
Mugs (units)	14,500	15,200	16,100	1, 400

    Revenues are expected to occur evenly throughout each period.

    Each mug costs 60p to make and is sold for £1.45.

    Inventory at the start of period 1 is 2,900 mugs. Inventory is now to be maintained at a level sufficient to cover four days of the next period's expected sales units.

    Required

    (a) Prepare the production budget in units for each of the periods 1–3.
    (b) Explain two benefits for Svetlana's business of introducing a system of budgetary control, rather than use a fixed production level.
    (c) Prepare an extract from the income statement for periods 1–3 to show the gross profit.

5   Vassilya owns a business manufacturing a single product.

    Her production for the first four months is expected to be as follows.

	Month 1	Month 2	Month 3	Month 4
Production in units	800	1,050	1,350	1,650

    Each unit takes 2.5 hours to manufacture. The workers are paid £8 per hour and £11 per hour when working overtime. There are 75 workers, who work 40 hours each a week.

Vassilya is pleased with the increase in production which has resulted from an expected increase in sales units, but is concerned with the extra labour costs arising through overtime being paid.

(a)   Prepare a labour budget to calculate the number of hours needed to fulfil expected production and the cost of labour, including the cost of overtime.

Vassilya does not want any spare capacity and wants her workers to work a fully productive month so that inventory can be produced in advance in preparation for the increased sales units in months 3 and 4.

(b)   Prepare a labour budget that maximises production without using overtime. Identify the production in units and the hours needed. Identify whether there is a surplus or deficit in production at the end of period 4 if overtime is not used.

(c)   Calculate the saving in costs if there is no spare capacity (compare the budgets in (a) to (b)).

6   AQA ACC4 June 2007 (adapted)

Damir Ltd is a small business that manufactures toys.

The following information is available for the next four months.

	January	February	March	April
Expected sales units	2,000	2,200	2,300	2,200

Additional information:

(a)   Each unit sells for £15.

(b)   Each month, 20% of revenue is expected to be on a cash basis.

(c)   Fifty per cent of trade receivables are expected to pay after one month. The remainder are expected to pay after two months.

(d)   Trade receivables on 1 January are expected to be:

  ▪ £21,600 from December revenue, of which £10,800 will be paid in January and the balance in February

  ▪ £7,200 from November revenue, which will be paid in January.

Required

Prepare a receivables budget for Damir Ltd for *each* of the four months January to April.

7   Stares Ltd produce and sell one product.

The expected sales units for periods 4–7 are:

	Period 4	Period 5	Period 6	Period 7
Sales units	2,000	2,200	2,400	2,800

Each unit sells for £25.

The opening inventory at the start of period 4 was 200 units.

Closing inventory is maintained at 10% of next month's expected sales units.

(a)   Prepare a sales (revenue) budget for periods 4–6.

(b)   Prepare a production budget for periods 4–6.

The standard cost per unit is 2 metres of material at £2.50 per metre and 1.5 hours of labour at £8 per hour.

(c)   Prepare a purchases budget to show the cost of raw materials for periods 4–6.

(d)   Prepare a labour budget to show the cost of labour for the periods 4–6.

(e)   Prepare a budgeted income statement to show the gross profit for the periods 4–6. Assume that inventory is valued at the standard cost.

The company pays for 60% of all purchases one month after purchase. The rest is paid for two months after purchase. The cost of purchases in period 3 was £8,000 and the cost of purchases in period 2 was £6,000.

(f)   Prepare a trade payables budget for the periods 4–6. Explain how information from this budget will be used in the statement of financial position (balance sheet).

16 Social accounting

In this chapter you will learn how to:

- explain the term 'social accounting'

- demonstrate an awareness of non-financial factors to be considered in decision-making

- make critical assessments of decisions from ethical and non-financial standpoints.

Key terms

Social accounting: this term is applied when businesses are accountable to society at large, whereby they must consider both the non-financial and financial aspects of every decision they make.

Stakeholders: any group or individual who has an interest in the activities of the business.

Show the skills

Sometimes it is difficult to ascertain which factors are financial and which are non-financial as it is often believed that all the decisions that a business makes are in the end financial as they will affect profitability. In general if figures are given, any use of these figures will give a financial argument and any ethical assessment is non-financial.

So far you have learnt about both financial accounting, for example the drawing up of the financial statements and statement of financial position (balance sheet) of different business structures, and management and cost accounting, for example the various budgets within budgetary control. Both of these include financial calculations. But accounting decisions are not based on financial implications alone as non-financial implications need to be considered as well before a decision can be made. This chapter deals with those non-financial considerations.

Case study

Mihail Danov

Mihail Danov is considering buying an outlet in a rural area. Previously the outlet was used as a farm store. Mihail intends to expand the building into a plastics factory which will enable him to increase his output by 20% and thereby increase profits in the long term once the costs of set-up have been covered. The new factory will include a large chimney that will expel pollution into the air. He will have to apply to the local council for permission to expand but believes he will be successful as the new factory will bring employment to the local area.

Social accounting

Social accounting is the term used to describe social accountability, whereby businesses must consider the non-financial as well as the financial aspects of any decisions that they make. It is argued that businesses must not be driven by the motive of profit maximisation alone, but must also consider the wider aspects of each decision. Consideration must be given as to how internal decisions can also affect external **stakeholders**, such as the local community, the workforce, the environment and society at large. Social accounting recognises that any business which fails to consider the accountability to society of its decisions may find that some of those decisions are counter-productive and that profitability falls as society responds negatively to their actions. One example would be the bad publicity given by the media to some of the petrol companies, accusing them of causing environmental damage to the sea and sea life by having defective and leaking pipes, which resulted in Greenpeace action and boycotting of the companies' petrol garages on publicised days. Similarly, an unhappy workforce may cause a fall in productivity if they perceive that the company is trying to save money by failing to maintain health and safety standards.

■ **Illustration**

How to write a report that includes non-financial considerations

Write a report to Mihail explaining the financial and non-financial considerations of his decision to expand the rural outlet.

To: Mihail Danov

From: Student

Date: Date of examination

Subject: An analysis of the implications of expanding the rural outlet

This report could include the following.

Financial considerations:

- What is the cost of the expansion?
- How long will it take to complete the expansion?
- Will the market be able to sustain the increase in output? Will competitors react by decreasing their prices and entering a price war?
- How long will the business have to wait until profits are made? Does the business have to borrow the money to pay for the expansion? If so, what is the interest rate?
- What financial backing is needed for the finance? Will Mihail have to put up his own possessions as security for the loan?
- Will there be any costs to consider if legal action is taken against the business because of the pollution?

Non-financial considerations:

- Will Mihail have to pay for a change of purpose for the farm store to be expanded into a factory? If so, how long will this take and can it be guaranteed?
- Will the local infrastructure be adequate for the increase in transport etc.?
- Are there transport links for the workforce to be able to travel to work? If not, are there a sufficient number of people for the workforce in the local area? Does the local community have enough skilled workers?
- What damage can pressure groups, for example environmentalists, do to the reputation of the business? Will they be able to stop or hinder the activities of the business in any way, for example by picketing outside the factory?
- Are there any legal implications of knowingly polluting the air?
- Will there be restrictions on the activities, for example only using the chimney between certain hours?
- How is the local community expected to react? Will there be petitions against the chimney and bad press?

■ **Explanatory note**

The report does not include any benefits of the expansion to the local community as the question only asks for considerations from Mihail's point of view. These could only be included if they resulted in good publicity for Mihail.

Study tip

A question on social accounting is to be expected in the examination paper. Although not guaranteed, often a question requires a report or prose answer to a scenario considering both the financial and non-financial aspects from the point of view of a particular stakeholder. Remember that although there is not a definite right or wrong answer, the examiner is looking for an evaluative answer that looks at both sides of the argument and comes to a final judgement.

Recommendation:

It appears that there could be considerable costs associated with expansion. It is recommended that investigations are made into whether a factory site can be found in a more urban area or whether an alternative production method can be used that does not necessitate the use of a chimney that causes pollution. It is recommended that Mihail does not buy the outlet until more consideration has been given to alternatives.

Examples of possible social accounting scenarios

Table 1 *Social accounting scenarios*

Scenario	Stakeholders affected	Possible considerations
New machine or plant that causes pollution	Employees	Ill health, refusal to work or train to use the new machine, strike action
	Local community	Drop in house prices, residents moving away, decline in area
	Environmental pressure groups	Bad publicity, picketing, boycotting product
	Owners (shareholders)	Bad publicity reducing share prices
Staff made redundant and replaced by robotics	Employees	Loss of jobs, remaining employees demotivated as fearful of losing their own jobs, low morale
	Banks/lenders	Concerns over cost of redundancies, security of loans
	Owners	Bad publicity in short term but hope of future profits
	Local community	Local unemployment, decline in area as workers move away to search for employment
	Trade unions	May take action to prevent job losses
Introduction of cheaper harmful product to product range	Customers	May refuse to buy and look to competitors
	Workforce	May refuse to work because of health concerns
	Suppliers	May have reputation harmed by association
	Owners (shareholders)	Bad publicity may reduce share price
	Trade unions	May take action on employees' behalf
	Pressure groups	Bad publicity, picketing, boycotting product
	Competitors	May underprice to increase market share

These are only some examples from a very wide range of possible scenarios.

Study tip

Always ensure that answers are from the perspective asked for in the question. For example, if the question asks the student to evaluate a business decision from the workforce's point of view, then there are no marks for answering from the owners' point of view. This will achieve no marks, however valid the comments. This also applies to general comments! Always relate comments to the scenario given in the question.

Activity

1 In the class form two groups of four students with the rest of the class as an audience. Decide on a topical business proposal. One group is to think of the financial arguments for going ahead with the proposal. The other group is to think of the non-financial factors against the decision. Both groups are to present their arguments to the rest of the class. The class is to make a final decision as to whether the proposal is to go ahead. This activity could be expanded so that different people consider the proposal from the viewpoint of different stakeholders.

In this chapter you will have learnt:

- the term 'social accounting'
- how to demonstrate an awareness of non-financial factors to be considered in decision-making
- how to make critical assessments of decisions from ethical and non-financial standpoints.

Practice questions

1   List four different stakeholders for the following businesses:
   (a)   an international manufacturing company
   (b)   a local takeaway restaurant
   (c)   a self-employed gardener.

2   Explain the meaning of the term 'social accounting' and its relevance to business decisions.

3   AQA ACC4 June 2007 (adapted)
   Describe the financial and non-financial factors that need to be considered before investing in a new expensive automated factory from the viewpoint of:
   (a)   the current workforce
   (b)   the shareholders
   (c)   competitors
   (d)   the local community.

4   AQA ACC7 June 2004 (adapted)
   Brent and Brodie are the directors in BB Ltd which trades in cosmetics made from ingredients not tested on animals. These ingredients are due to rise in price by 40% over the next six months.
   Brodie has proposed a change in supplier. The new supplier is from overseas and will decrease the present cost of ingredients by 10%; however, they test their ingredients on animals. Brent is unsure as to how their customers will react to the proposed change in supplier, but Brodie insists that they will prefer cheaper prices.
   Write a brief report to Brent and Brodie considering the effect of the proposed change in supplier on:
   (a)   present customers
   (b)   competitors
   (c)   ordinary shareholders.

5   Wenbo Zhang is considering investing £40,000 of his savings into ordinary shares in Claxon plc, a successful UK manufacturing company. The directors of Claxon plc have recently discovered that the company's main supplier uses cheap child labour in a Third World country. This supplier has received very negative media coverage in the UK. If the company changes supplier production costs are expected to rise considerably.
   Write a report to Wenbo Zhang as to whether he should invest his money into Claxon plc.

Glossary

A

Accounting standard: this allows financial statements to be compiled in a format that allows them to be compared over years and between companies.

Adjustment for goodwill: when a partner joins or leaves a partnership a change to goodwill is made according to the partners' profit sharing ratios.

Adverse variance: the actual figures are worse than the standard figures in the budget, resulting in a lower actual profit than was expected.

Allocation: the process of charging costs which derive from a cost centre directly to that particular cost centre.

Analysts: their job is to closely examine trends, published accounts and the **Stock Exchange** where stocks and shares are bought and sold and make predictions.

Annual general meeting (AGM): the yearly meeting of a limited company to which all the shareholders are invited.

Apportionment: the process of charging overhead costs to a cost centre on a rational basis.

Appropriation account: this account records the distribution of profits among partners based on any agreement made by the partners. Where there is no agreement the terms of the Partnership Act 1890 should be applied. The account includes interest on drawings, interest on capital, partnership salaries and the share of the residual profit or loss.

Auditors: are accountants independent of the limited company and are responsible for the checking of the accounts to give an opinion as to whether they provide a 'true and fair view'. They work on behalf of the shareholders.

AVCO: the weighted average cost method involves a new value of inventory being calculated each time a different cost is paid. This new cost is then used for issues until a new receipt of inventory is made.

B

Bank loans: borrowing a fixed sum over a fixed term which can be secured on assets in the business or unsecured. Interest must be paid in addition to the amount borrowed.

Bank overdrafts: represent a flexible source of finance and mean a business can spend more than they have in their bank account within a set limit.

Break-even point: the point at which total revenue equals total costs and so neither a profit nor a loss is made.

Budget: a financial plan for the future expressed in quantitative terms. It is used to control the use of resources so that the business objectives can be achieved.

Budget centre: a department or area for which a budget has been set up.

Budgetary control: where responsibility to achieve the budget has been delegated to the budget centre managers.

Budgeting: the preparation of the budgets.

C

Capital deficiency: occurs when a partner has insufficient funds in their account to cover the loss of the dissolution.

Capital investment appraisal: the process of using cash flows to decide whether a capital project should be undertaken.

Cash and cash equivalents (bank and cash): cash held in the business and/or in the bank account.

Cash inflows: movements of cash into the company such as a share issue or sale of non-current assets.

Cash outflows: movements of cash out of the company, e.g. repaying loans or purchasing non-current assets.

Companies Act 1985, amended 1989 and 2006: this Act governs limited companies and requires that limited companies prepare and publish accounts annually. In 1989 EU directives (rules imposed by the European Union to harmonise accounting) were added.

Contribution: the money available to pay fixed costs and then once they are paid contribution becomes profit.

Cost centre: a production or service location whose costs may be attributed to cost units, e.g. a production department.

Cost driver: the factors that cause costs of an activity and also cause these costs to change.

Cost of capital: the discounting factor used in capital investment appraisals to discount future cash flows so that they are equivalent in value to cash now.

Cost pool: the location of a group of related indirect costs.

Cost unit: a unit of production or service that absorbs the cost centre's overheads costs, e.g. a product such as a television set or a service such as a restaurant meal.

Cost variance: the difference between the standard cost and the actual cost.

Current account: records all the partners' drawings, interest on drawings, interest on capital, partnership salaries and shares of residual profit or loss.

D

Debentures: these are loans by debenture holders who receive interest for the term of the debenture. They must not be confused with shares.

Deed of partnership: this is a legal document. Ideally all partnerships should have one of these so they know exactly how profits will be shared etc.

Direct costs: this cost is identified with the cost unit. Costs attributable to a particular product, e.g. direct materials and direct labour.

Directors: are appointed by the shareholders to run the business and must produce a report as part of the published accounts. They are responsible for producing the financial statements.

Dissolution: this takes place when a partnership ceases to continue operating. It could be because the partners want this to happen or are forced to because of problems such as lack of cash and/or profit.

Dividends: the reward to the shareholders for investing. It is not guaranteed that dividends will be paid if there is insufficient cash or profit.

F

Factory profit, or manufacturing profit: the difference between the transfer price and the production cost of completed goods, or the amount of markup.

Favourable variance: the actual figures are better than the standard figures in the budget resulting in a higher actual profit than was expected.

FIFO: the first in first out method involves the oldest costs being used first when inventory is issued.

Financing activities: changes in the equity capital and borrowings.

Finished goods: fully completed goods.

Fixed capital accounts: the amount of capital introduced or withdrawn by each partner is recorded in a separate account and does not alter unless agreed by the partnership.

Fixed cost: these costs do not vary with the level of production.

Flexed budget: amending standard costs for changes in levels of production.

Forecast financial statements: the forecast income statement and statement of financial position (balance sheet) based on the functional budgets contained within the master budget.

Full cost: the production cost of each cost unit and includes both direct and indirect costs.

G

Garner v. Murray: this case set the precedent that if one partner cannot pay his or her share of capital deficiency then the other partners must cover the amount according to their most recent capital account ratio.

Goodwill: reflects the reputation built up by a partnership, this is an intangible asset and there are several different approaches to valuing it, but it is essentially a reflection of the success of the partnership. This could be based on previous profits for example. It could also represent the difference between the net assets of the partnership and the amount the partnership could be sold for.

I

IAS 1 Presentation of Financial Statements: sets out overall requirements for the presentation of financial statements.

IAS 2 Inventories: concerned with inventory as an asset and expense and how it is valued.

IAS 7 Statement of Cash Flows: the International Accounting Standard we need to follow using the indirect method. It provides information about changes in cash and cash equivalents (bank and cash), using the indirect method.

IAS 8 Accounting Policies, Changes in Accounting Estimates and Errors: criteria for selecting and changing accounting policies.

IAS 10 Events After the Reporting Period: these events may affect users' interpretation of the financial statements.

IAS 16 Property, Plant and Equipment: concerns tangible assets held for more than one accounting period and used in the production or supply of goods and services, or for administration.

IAS 18 Revenue: includes revenue from sale of goods, rendering of services and use by others of

entity assets yielding interest, royalties and dividends.

IAS 36 Impairment of Assets: an asset must not be shown at more than the highest amount to be recovered through its use or sale.

IAS 37 Provisions, Contingent Liabilities and Contingent Assets: aims to ensure that appropriate measurement and recognition criteria are applied to assist users.

IAS 38 Intangible Assets: non-monetary assets without physical substance.

Income statement: this term replaces the trading, profit and loss account.

Indirect costs: this cost is not identified with the cost unit. Costs that cannot be attributed to a particular product, e.g. indirect labour such as the wages of supervisory staff.

Indirect method: profit or loss is adjusted to determine operating cash flow.

Interest on capital: this is an appropriation of the profits of the partnership and rewards those partners who have invested most.

Interest on drawings: in order to deter partners from taking excessive drawings there may be interest charged that is then debited to the partners' accounts.

Internal finance: often the first source of finance for a business to consider and involves freeing up cash within the business.

International Accounting Standard: standards set by the International Accounting Standards Board.

Inventories: raw materials, work in progress or finished goods.

Investing activities: acquisition and disposal of non-current assets and investment property (investments) that are not cash equivalents.

J

JIT: just in time is an increasingly popular method of handling inventory where the minimum amount of inventory is held and replenished as required.

L

Labour budget: shows the expected amount of labour hours and the resulting cost of labour based on the production budget.

Labour efficiency variance: the difference between the actual hours used and the standard hours expected to be used, at the standard rate paid.

Labour intensive: the production or service location has more direct labour hours than machine hours.

Labour rate variance: the difference between the actual rate paid per hour and the standard rate expected to be paid, for the actual hours used.

M

Machine intensive: the production or service location has more direct machine hours than labour hours. The location can otherwise be known as capital intensive.

Manufacturing account: an account prepared to calculate the production cost of manufactured goods.

Manufacturing overheads: the indirect costs incurred in the production of the products, e.g. depreciation of machinery, factory insurance and factory rent. These are often known as factory overheads.

Marginal cost: the cost of one extra unit.

Margin of safety: the difference between the number of sales units achieved (or maximum output) and the number of units at the break-even point, where the amount of sales achieved must exceed the break-even point otherwise a loss is made.

Master budget: taken from the functional budgets and consists of a budgeted income statement and forecast statement of financial position (balance sheet).

Material price variance: the difference between the actual price paid and the standard price expected to be paid, for the actual materials used.

Material usage variance: the difference between the actual materials used and the standard materials expected to be used, at the standard price paid.

Mortgages: long-term loans specifically for purchasing property (premises).

N

Net cash from operating activities: profit from operations is adjusted for movements in trade receivables, inventories, etc. to obtain this figure.

Net present value: a capital investment appraisal method that uses the present value of net cash inflows to ascertain whether the capital project should be undertaken on financial grounds.

Non-current assets: the term used for assets that are expensive items bought not primarily to resell but to help generate profits and keep for longer than one financial year, e.g. property (premises) and machinery.

Non-current liabilities: what the company owes and has a repayment date of longer than 12 months such as a loan or debentures.

O

Operating activities: revenue-producing activities that are not investing or financing.

Ordinary shares: these are the most common type of share issued. An ordinary shareholder receives a variable dividend based on profit in return for their investment.

Over-absorption: occurs when more units are produced than was predicted in the budget and therefore more overheads are absorbed into the cost unit.

Overhead absorption rate (OAR): the rate which is used to absorb the overheads into the cost unit. It is calculated as either rate per direct machine hour or rate per direct labour hour depending on which the department uses the most.

P

Partnership Act 1890: this states, for example how to share profits or losses if no agreement is in place.

Partnership salary: this is a payment to a partner and appears in the appropriation section, not with expenses. It is also entered in the partner's current account. It may reflect that some partners may contribute more working hours than others.

Payback: a calculation of how long it takes to generate enough cash inflows to cover the initial cost of a capital project.

Periodic method: this is when inventory is valued at the end of a financial period. It is the quickest method and should always be used when calculating the FIFO method even when perpetual is asked for as the same answer is found.

Perpetual method: a running balance is kept using this method and a new value of inventory is calculated each time inventory is received or issued.

Potential investors: are people who may wish to buy shares in a company. The element of risk and potential reward is important to this group and also whether they intend to invest for the short or long term.

Preference shares: for shareholders these are a lower risk option than ordinary shares but as a consequence offer a lower return.

Prime costs: the total of all direct costs incurred when producing the products.

Production budget: the calculation of expected production in units based on the information from the sales (revenue) budget and accounting for movements in inventory of finished goods.

Production cost of manufactured goods (also known as 'cost of production' or 'production cost of completed goods'): the total of all the costs of manufacturing the products.

Production department: where the product is actually made, e.g. the machining department.

Purchases budget: a calculation of the expected value of purchases of materials based on the production levels as shown by the production budget.

R

Realisation account: used to close the partnership and calculate the profit or loss for the partners once all the assets have been sold or taken over.

Retirement of a partner: a structural change to the partnership and creates a 'new' partnership as a result. When a partner decides to retire we need to calculate the latest profit, the current worth of the partnership and perhaps reward the retiring partner for goodwill built up.

Revaluation account: non-current assets such as property (premises) will have normally increased in value but others may have decreased such as inventory. This account records the changes in value.

Risk: all lenders have to decide on the level of risk a business presents. This is based on past experience, future predictions and on the current state of the business. The lender must decide how likely they are to be repaid and whether the likely return is worth the potential risk. In the role of the borrower, the business also has to weigh up the risks of any source of finance. The business must consider its financial needs, as well as the implications associated with each source.

Royalties: a sum of money paid to the inventor of a product for the right of use of his ideas.

S

Sale or return: goods are supplied and do not need to be paid for until they are sold and can be returned to the supplier if they don't sell.

Sales price variance: the difference between the actual selling price per product and the standard selling price expected per product, for the actual units sold.

Sales (revenue) budget: a summary of the expected sales units and sales value for the future.

Sales (revenue) variance: the difference between the standard revenue and actual revenue.

Sales volume variance: the difference between the actual number of units sold and the standard number of units expected to be sold, at the standard selling price.

Schedule of non-current assets: this records the movement/revaluation (purchase and sale) of non-current assets and the depreciation attached to the movements.

Semi-variable costs: these costs are partly fixed and partly variable.

Service department: these departments support the other departments, e.g. technical support and canteen.

Social accounting: this term is applied when businesses are accountable to society at large, whereby they must consider both the non-financial and financial aspects of every decision they make.

Stakeholders: any group or individual who has an interest in the activities of the business.

Standard cost: a predetermined cost that should be achieved through an efficient working environment.

Standard cost card: specifies the standard costs predetermined for one unit.

Standard costing: the preparation and use of standard costs, including the calculation of variances.

Statement of affairs: a basic statement of financial position (balance sheet) that can be used to calculate missing figures such as profit, loss, opening or closing capital.

Statement of cash flows: this shows how cash has been generated (cash inflows) and how it has been spent (cash outflows), information not provided by the income statement or statement of financial position (balance sheet).

Statement of changes in equity: this section records the issue of shares, revaluation of non-current assets, bonus issues of shares and payment of dividends.

Statement of financial position: this term replaces the balance sheet.

Stock Exchange: this is where stocks and shares are bought and sold, mainly second-hand shares and government securities.

Sub-variance: each total variance can be broken down into two sub-variances that analyse the reasons for the variance in more detail.

T

Time value of money: this concept states that money received or paid out in the future does not have the same value as money today.

Trade and other receivables (prepayments): this includes trade receivables and other receivables (prepayments), amounts owed to the business or that the business have paid for in advance, e.g. rent and insurance.

Trade and other payables (accruals): this includes trade payables and other trade payables (accruals), what the business owes to trade creditors.

Trade payables budget: a summary of the expected movement in money owed by the business to the suppliers.

Trade receivables budget: a summary of the expected movement in money owed by the customers to the business.

Transfer price: production cost of completed goods plus a percentage markup.

U

Under-absorption: this occurs when fewer units are produced than was predicted in the budget and therefore not all the overheads are absorbed into the cost unit.

Unrealised profit on finished goods: profit that is not recognised until the inventory is sold and a contract of sale has been negotiated.

V

Variable cost: these costs vary with the level of production.

Variance: the difference between a standard cost or revenue and an actual cost or revenue.

W

Work in progress: partly finished goods.

Index

Key terms are in **bold**.